To dearest Robin,
Worth reading for a few hints.
Love Nalini
Xmas 1988.

A
MARRIAGE
SURVIVAL
GUIDE

By the same author

A Parents' Survival Guide

fiction
The Man for the Job

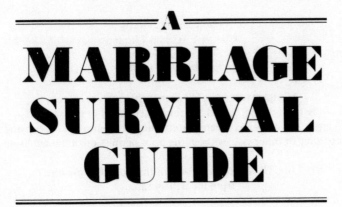

A MARRIAGE SURVIVAL GUIDE

LAURIE GRAHAM

with cartoons by
Gray Jolliffe

Chatto & Windus
LONDON

Published in 1988 by
Chatto & Windus Limited
30 Bedford Square
London WC1B 3RP

A CIP catalogue record for this book is available
from the British Library.

ISBN 0 7011 3399 6

Typeset at The Spartan Press Ltd,
Lymington, Hants
Printed in Great Britain by
Redwood Burn Ltd,
Trowbridge, Wiltshire

Contents

This book is dedicated to David,
my co-pilot for sixteen years.

Twelve Things That Baffle Husbands

- Knitting
- Capo di Monte
- Quiche
- Rubber gloves
- Throwing things away, especially unidentified washers and sump oil
- Piped rosettes
- Tupperware parties
- Gynaecology
- Laura Ashley
- Panty hose
- Panty hose worn with knickers
- Shopping

And Twelve Things They Just Don't Like

- Weddings
- Royal Weddings
- Tears
- Your best friend
- Sherry
- Small dogs
- Gateau
- Heated rollers
- Soft centres
- Barry Manilow
- Blood
- The inside of handbags

A Dozen Things Wives Don't Like

- Things that go bang
- Your best friend
- You admiring her best friend
- Work benches
- Sausage, kidneys, liver, brains, lungs, and two eggs
  sunny side up
- The internal combustion engine
- The internal combustion engine in pieces
- Surprise guests
- Mice
- Anything in black and red satin with underwiring and
  four suspenders
- Dirt
- Men who talk back

And A Dozen More They Can't See The Point Of

- Ten pints of lager
- Boxing
- Prize vegetables that are not for eating
- Poker
- 38D-cup centrefolds
- Accumulator bets
- Eskimo Nell
- Fishing
- Batting averages
- Billiards
- Many other things involving balls
- TA Weekend Manoeuvres

1

Married is Better

There's a long line of reasons for getting married. Moral reasons. Financial reasons. For security. Children. Sex without having to go looking for it. Because you said you would after five Martinis and you always keep your promises. We could go on all night. Whatever other excuses we have, most of us marry for one simple reason. We don't want to be alone.

Alone is a very unnerving thing to be. Especially if you wake up and find you're twenty years older, independent, busy busy busy, and frightened by the sound of your own breathing. Alone, there is no one to make you do the things you hate. No one to stop your misguided enjoyment of the things you love. Decisions about the wallpaper, the room temperature, God, and what to eat for dinner, are entirely your own. Alone, you may even decide to give dinner a miss. This is how civilisations collapse.

To be alone as little as possible is a great human obsession. How else do you explain Torremolinos? Okay, when some lone yachtsperson reaches the far shore, we all say, 'Didn't he do well!' and maybe buy a commemorative tea towel, but the consensus amongst right-thinking people is that he must have had a button missing to set sail in the first place. Right-thinking people aspire to be half of a couple. Even in the middle of the Atlantic.

Coupledom

What is a couple? Depends where you're standing. It's a biological imperative, for one thing. But that need only take a few minutes. Still, if you're going to pair up for babies, why not for companionship, interior decoration, and life everlasting?

To the reluctantly single, coupledom is an enviable state. To those who are single and like it, coupledom is a tyranny. Their world is full of couples who, publicly at least, speak with one voice. A half-couple, in isolation from its other half, will opine and debunk and complain until the cows come home. But bring the other half within earshot and the tune changes. They nod and smile and ennoble a tedious story they've heard a hundred times before, because to withdraw that kind of support *in public* is not a very married thing to do.

Socially, couples see singles as renegades. Their lifestyles hint at space, time, choices . . . They may be dangerous. At best they are dinner party spares.

Individually we may be raving neurotics, but sympathetically paired off, our neuroses become contented normality. Let me show you what I mean. A spinster with a house full of cats and six locks on her door. Can *that* be normal? Put a husband and wife in the same circumstances and what have you got? A pair of security-conscious cat lovers, that's what. Safety in numbers, you see?

Advanced Coupledom

Togetherness is an advanced form of coupledom.

In days of old when knights were bold and there was no bonking on Sundays, Fridays and the forty days of Lent, there wasn't a lot of it about. Even thirty years ago, if a couple had announced, 'We *do* like to *do* things together' people would have turned away in embarrassment. Nowadays everybody's doing it. You can even buy books to advise you how. I just read one and it said: *In order to have a fulfilling relationship with your partner you must give him your exclusive attention on a regular, scheduled basis.* This is a dangerous, inward-looking way to carry on. Togetherness is the hardest balancing act in the world. If one of you moves an inch, to scratch your nose, or change your opinion, the other has to move too. You may only have wanted to get out from under, one evening a week for a guitar lesson, but what have you done? Blown it, that's all! You are my world, you're every breath I take . . . Nice tune, shame about the words.

Terminal Coupledom

Look, we shall get nowhere without plain speaking. Acute togetherness is usually caused by women.

We all have things we prefer other people to take care of. Like where the rent is coming from. And tomorrow's clean shirt. And what we are going to do with our lives. Men are very good at making assumptions about the laundry. Women make a speciality out of saying, 'Why don't you come home a bit earlier and take up all this slack in my life?'

She wants togetherness. He wants a clean shirt. When a man marries, the shape of his life hardly changes at all. Most of them become married bachelors. But when a woman becomes a wife, she re-defines herself. If Roger likes long hair, no nail varnish, dinner on the table at six, and not to be bothered with womanly details like curtain material and hysterectomies, that is how Jane models herself for marriage. She grows her hair. Lies awake half the night with curtains on her mind. And dwindles. Is there any married woman out there who can put her hand on her heart and say *she's* not dwindled?

Hunt The Slipper

The usual prelude to Western marriage is romantic love. This is rather like preparing to be assistant stage manager of Hartlepool Rep by being an overnight Broadway sensation.

Romantic love is a roller-coaster ride. One minute intensely wonderful, the next minute intensely not. Marriage is something opposite. It has to be. Its basis is habit and familiarity, often likened to a pair of old slippers. The difficult exercise the about-to-be-married has to perform is to get off the roller-coaster, look at the bearer of red roses and sweet valentines, and ask the question, 'Is *this* Old Slipper material?'

Umm... I'll need time to think it over Richard — but since you're down there can you check if Timmy's ball is stuck under the sofa?

How can you tell? You can't. You can only listen to instinct, listen to your friends, *for Chrissakes listen to your friends*, and then cross your fingers. It takes two old slippers to make a pair, and it takes time. A couple who marry today will have plenty of that. If they don't divorce, they can expect to spend forty or fifty years together. And that's a very long time, isn't it? In the past, death must have solved an awful lot of problems.

Apparently, the longer you stay married the less likely you are to divorce. Not only that, but some marriages actually improve with keeping. Other people simply run out of energy for making major changes in their lives. And for many couples an endured marriage is seen as a possible stepping stone to heaven. A case of 'We started this, so we'll finish, and anyway, whoever said it'd be fun?' In people married for fifty years this is not a surprising philosophy. But I have encountered it as early as one year into a marriage. Man and wife rubbing along in honourable misery.

Divorce continues to get a bad press. Admissions of failure and brave attempts to unglue mistakes always attract snipers. Their condemnation is based on the bizarre logic that the best thing to do on a sinking ship is put your name down for a game of deck quoits.

Most of us choose our own partners. Most of us get what we deserve. And here we are, in the up-front, raised consciousness, communicate or bust Eighties, with most wives still perceiving husbands as Great Dane puppies – naughty, ridiculous, and irresistible. And most husbands perceiving wives as Matron – formidable, kill-joy, and . . . irresistible. No change. In spite of the emergence of the New Man and the Un-dependent Woman, most marriages bear more than a passing resemblance to an Andy Capp cartoon. To be honest, I have never met New Man or Un-dependant Woman. Have you? Someone told me there have been corroborated sightings in parts of London, but I'm not getting excited. I've heard too many stories about the Yeti.

Twelve Six I must be able to find Three Good Reasons For Getting Married

1 You can stop holding in your stomach

2 You can fart and not blame the dog

3 When your very best friend calls late and asks you to make up a four with some terrifically attractive, not to mention humorous, sincere and individuated person who has bad breath and should be granted a free transfer from the human race, you can say NO.

2

What Every Growing Boy Should Know

Long ago and far away there were two sorts of women. Those who would, and those who wouldn't, unless you married them, and then they would sometimes. Life was simple. You lusted after the ones who would, and found yourself one of the others to be mother to your children. And you were not likely to make a mistake. Trash was trash. Shameless Jezebels did not read *Bride* magazine. And if you were in any doubt at all, you could always check with your mother.

Then, one Thursday morning, the feminist revolution happened. Women started doing things that were unheard of. Hailing their own cabs. Buying men drinks. Instead of a world of sluts and bimbos, village bikes, totty, skirt, fiancées, wives, mothers, saints, saintly mothers and blessed martyrs, there were just women. As if this wasn't bad enough, some of them went on to become wimmin, but that turned out to be a very small blip on the screen. It is enough to say the name *woman* developed a hard edge.

There was then a lot of noise and fuss because consciousnesses were being raised. A lot of women got very excited and exhilarated and a lot of men got very disappointed and confused. The ones who were old enough to remember the good old days went into deep shock, and the ones who were just out of short trousers were very annoyed. They had been looking forward to a few years of floozy followed by a lifetime of free laundry. A wonderful party was over and they hadn't even had time to take off their coats and find a glass.

It was a terrible time to be a man. There were no certainties any more. And there was a feeling in the air that once the worst of the upheaval had been weathered, on some issues there could be no going back. Women would never again be quite what they used to be.

Or would they? Wasn't something being overlooked? Wasn't there an element, somewhere at the heart of every woman, that hadn't changed at all? Weren't there a lot of women, even up there in the revolutionary vanguard, who were faking it? Of course there were. See chaps? Things are hardly ever as bad as they seem. It takes more than a bit of Germaine Greer to change the inner woman.

It touches a nerve in me to speak of this, but we must. To understand it is central to understanding nearly everything that happens in a relationship between a man and a woman. I am talking about the **Twinkie Tendency**.

The **Twinkie Tendency** is a psychological knot in the wood. It enables one woman to be a ball-breaking negotiator and a sweet compliant child, all at the same time. It is a very rare woman indeed who is not tainted by it. To say this in the 1980s is a kind of blasphemy. Any man who even hints at it will find himself committed in shackles to the deepest sty in a male chauvinist piggery. And from the lips of an actual woman it constitutes a capital offence. I could get lynched for thinking about it. But it is true.

What Is A Twinkie?

A **Twinkie** is a child-woman. Twinkiedom is the dream of being looked after. Its enticing messages are whispered in a little girl's ear from the day she is born. 'Freedom is frightening. *Everything* is frightening. Stay here where you're safe. Let someone else go and check for monsters.' After years of listening to this siren song is it any wonder women go to such lengths to avoid growing up? Is it any wonder they have developed such ingenious techniques for not being responsible for themselves? They will worm the cat, scrub the lavatory, and quite literally pick up any soiled gauntlet thrown down to them, as long as someone else will ensure they can live comfortably ever after.

If a man will just do that one small thing – and after all, isn't that what men are raised to do? – she will take upon herself domestic shittiness in all its forms, and she will show him a kind of deference, because he is her keeper. But it will only be a kind of deference. There will be a strong under-current of suppressed fury, because being kept has its disadvantages.

Here is the bind Twinkies find themselves in. They want to play with the grown-ups, but they don't want to part with the stake-money. Many wives are little girls in high heels. Emotionally they have been On Hold since about the age of twelve. Superficially they look fine. They may have careers and opinions and their own front door key. But if they are truthful, they are really just enjoying their turn in the Wendy House. And most husbands play along. 'That's all right,' they say. 'You wipe the tide-mark from round the bath, and I'll go and stand out on Mean Street and slay a few dragons. What's for tea?'

I'm A Twinkie, I'm a Twinkie
What Kind Of Twinkie Am I?

Twinkies come in a variety of forms. Many are covert, many are deluding themselves. One of the most emotionally honest women you can choose as a life partner is an **Unapologetic Twinkie**. That is, if you can't find one of the half dozen women in the whole of the charted universe that are not Twinkies at all. Bet you can't. Anyway, who'd want to live with a freak?

The Unapologetic Twinkie is very straightforward. She was

9

Daddy's little girl. She may still have a big teddy that sits by her pillow. Always check a girl for soft toys before you marry her.

This Twinkie is so easy to recognise. She is utterly without guile. Have you seen Orville the Duck? You've got it! This girl is a quacky, daffy, fluffy ducky ol' cutie pie. Her voice is a husky whimper. She'll probably make you very happy.

Feminists hate this travesty of sisterhood. To see her is to catch sight of a reflection you've been avoiding. She is without shame. She makes open deals with men. 'Look after me for ever' she lisps 'and I'll take care of the ring round your collar.' Many women refuse to play this crass, demeaning role. They prefer to operate with a little subtlety. A subtle Twinkie is a smart Twinkie.

Smart Twinkies are dangerous and confusing. They also represent an important section of female society. Probably the biggest. The chances of your not marrying a Smart Twinkie at some time in your life are very slender indeed.

She may be hard to spot, in the way that people who never miss *Dallas* are hard to spot – they look normal and they are *everywhere*. There used to be Sunday School Teachers and there used to be tramps who wore rouge. Now you just never know. A Smart Twinkie may not dress to titillate, she may not be inclined to cosset, and she may be unwilling to cajole, but her essential function in life is to make a man feel so desirable that he will pay the next gas bill. And the next. At first glance she may look like the perfect wife.

Smart Twinkies feel nothing but contempt for Unapologetic Twinkies. This is sheer professional jealousy. A Smart Twinkie is caught in a maelstrom of contradictions. On the one hand she wants to be a go-getter. On the other hand she wants a man to go get. And on the *other* hand, she wants to tell him exactly how she would do it, if she weren't so busy ducking out. Smart Twinkies always have three hands. That way they can keep one free to press the Twinkie button.

Her outward style may be very liberated. If she is a woman of honour she will try from time to time to grow up. She'll think, 'This is no way to carry on. What's a big girl like me doing in Maximum Security?' She may do her best, her almost best, to stop messing around and stand shoulder to shoulder with you through the storms of life, but the failure rate is depressingly high. Relapse into full-blooded Twinkiedom is almost inevitable. The best she may be able to achieve is a condition of compromise.

She may become an **Assertive Woman with Twinkie Leanings.** Here we have another con-merchant. This one lives on a see-saw. She would like to be conventionally passive. She would love to stand up and be counted with all the other ditzes.

But she read somewhere that this debasing lifestyle is a betrayal of womankind. So she makes an effort, asserts herself for five minutes and then, unnerved by the strange sensation of being a proper person, she retreats. Recognise her? Let me tell you one of her game-plans.

Assertive Woman is telling you something. She speaks confidently. She's coming across well. Authoritative, un-ambiguous. What's going on? Has she been hypnotised? Is she taking something? If she is, can she get you some in time for that meeting on Wednesday? No, no, no! She's just been reading some book on how to ask for a rise. Listen to her! This is terrific! She's sounding like a real man. There could be a field goal here! Ah . . . fumbled it. She had a clear run with a firm statement of intent, and she's bottled out. She's settled for a tentative enquiry. With a little shimmy of the shoulders, and a nice smile. Great! Don't you love her! She had it all set up to tell you how it is, and then right at the end, a little dip in the voice, a little shoulder, *so* and those three little words *don't you think?* The dead giveaway. Now do you recognise her? This is Assertive Woman with her Twinkie showing.

Now For The Good News

Any of these women can make you a good wife. It depends what you want.

If you crave the quiet life. If you will be happiest with a woman who asks only to be allowed to breathe and to please you, choose an Unapologetic Twinkie. There are still lots of them around, but be warned, they are so popular with men that there will always be a shortfall in supply. How about an alternative? How about a career girl with fully collapsible ambitions? How about a Smart Twinkie?

Or do you like to live on your nerves? If you hanker after the thrill of life on a switch-back, if you'll be satisfied by nothing less than the cut and thrust of marriage to an uncompromising marshmallow, go out and place an ad for an Assertive Woman with Twinkie Leanings.

Whoever you choose, be sure to mention early on in the relationship who else you will require her to be. This may seem obvious, but you'd be surprised how many men propose marriage, go through the ceremony and the honeymoon, and then drop the bombshell. 'Come on! It's been three weeks and you haven't been Mother Teresa for even five minutes!' If your marriage is to stand any chance of survival, you must come clean. 'Can you be Samantha Fox every Friday and Saturday, except the two weeks preceding the National Sales Conference? Also I'd like you to be Florence Nightingale, Sunday mornings as required. And Rin Tin Tin until further notice.'

All this should be discussed openly and frankly before you sign the register. Apart from anything else it will give her the opportunity to tell you what qualities she'll be looking out for in you.

3

Manwatching

All a woman looks for in a husband is that he be sensitive, exciting, strong, self-starting, and attentive. What *is* wrong with men today? They slob around. At most they manage to be one or two of those things at a time, and they wonder why women get irritable. Women are bound to get irritable. Any woman who has ever read *Cosmopolitan* has had a look round the sweet shop, so to speak. She wants a little of everything. She wants it in a size 15 shirt and a pair of trousers that *fit*.

Women often choose partners who have characteristics they wished they possessed themselves. By marrying someone who is apparently dynamic or charismatic, a woman may feel able to stay safely on the side-line and yet play out a vicarious part in the big bad world. This is one reason for choosing a particular husband, but there are many more. And before any woman chooses any man she should hold a certificate of competence in the study of The Nature of Man.

The Nature of Man

Human males who know what's good for them are pack animals. There are exceptions, of course. Men who reject pack life usually have a very hard time of it and end up writing poetry. Most men survive by having a little bit of **Packman** about them. Let me explain.

Pack mentality is what makes men join clubs. Do something for me. Go to the park and wait for a merry band of dogs to pass by. Watch what they do. They sniff lamp-posts. They stick together. Above all, they follow their leader. A dog without a leader is a basket case. He needs to go in a corner with his suckie blanket until another leader comes along.

Even a dog with a human minder is obsessed with this leadership thing. You may have him firmly on the end of a lead, but under his breath he's always muttering, '*She's* my leader. She *is* my leader. Remind me one more time, who's my leader?' Men are similar. They are happiest when they are strongly led. Margaret Thatcher is no accident of history.

This aspect of men is one of the hardest for women to comprehend. But you must. You must allow for it in all your calculations, even if you marry a very nice man indeed.

Let's talk about niceness. Most women, when asked, say all they want is a nice feller. Questioned more closely it turns out that at least half of them are fibbing. At least half of them perceive genuinely nice men as utter prats.

Niceman

Fact: there are nice men. Another fact: niceness is an easy thing to fake, in the short term. Beware of impostors. Even your mother may be fooled. You may bring home a barracuda in an Austin Reed blazer and just because he doesn't pick his nose in public (yet) she'll tell people, 'Barbara found a nice man at last. God willing I shall be a grandmother after all!'

But let's look on the bright side. Let's suppose you really do seem to have found the pukka thing. Adaptable, reasonable, vulnerable yet deeply resourceful . . . do I really have to carry on? There can only ever be one problem with a nice man. And that is boredom. This is the paradox of living with decent people. Niceness is not a very *stimulating* quality. Neither is Nearly-Niceness.

Nearly Niceman

This man is also known as **New Man**, although he's not so new as he used to be. Unlike really nice men, who were just born that way, this chap aspires towards niceness. One or two have had it thrust upon them. It's all to do with the changing role of women. Tell me what isn't.

Nearly Niceman has tried to become a better person. He has tried to shuffle off the stereotyping he grew up with. He's tried to open up and allow the gentler, feminine element of his psyche to flower. He really has tried. You almost feel obliged to like him. If only he weren't so whingeingly full of personal

16

insight. If only he'd stay late at the boozer sometimes. If only he weren't such a nerd.

This man would make a good partner if he could stop analysing every doubt, fear and need that crops up. If only he'd stop contemplating his own navel. Actually, if you look closely, you'll notice that it isn't his *navel* he's contemplating.

Handyman

This is a nice man with a power drill. The question is, can he handle it? Could you be marrying a man who is all talk and no fitted wardrobes? A real handyman can be a source of joy forever, but a duffer who won't admit that's what he is can be a liability. 'I'll just knock this wall down while I'm waiting for my dinner.' He probably will. And he'll just sever the gas mains, a public sewer, and a cable carrying 240,000 volts. You only wanted a washer changing on the kitchen tap. Never keep **Handyman** waiting for his dinner. You could end up with one large open-plan room and still nowhere to hang your coat. If you have the slightest suspicion, before you accept an engagement ring frisk him for wood chisels.

Then there are the Not So Nice Men –

Ratman And The Lone Ranger

Ratman knows there's a little girl one born every minute. Rats come in all shapes and sizes but one factor unites them. They are all front. In the Love and Devotion Game they never come up with the goods.

Women who are attracted to Ratman always believe it is within their power, and theirs alone, to turn him into Prince Charming. This is a mug's game. A woman can only keep a rat interested while he is in a state of anxious pursuit. The moment she lets slip some incriminating endearment, she's done for. Give a rat so much as a hint that you really care about him and you'll be left with nothing more than a rat-hole in your skirting board.

Lone Ranger is slightly different. He is tough, silent and blasé. For blasé, read aloof. For aloof, read terrified. Terrified to admit that something or someone is losing them sleep. Easier to play at being James Dean than to break down and admit they're in love. A Lone Ranger never depends, never softens, never trusts. Too risky.

Well-meaning women think, 'Aha! Here is a basically nice guy battling with the pain of old wounds. I'll just give him fifteen to twenty years of tender loving care and he'll be as right as ninepence!' Smart women whack his horse across the backside and let him gallop off into the sunset.

And finally, there are men who invite more pity than anger –

Peter Pan

I would not recommend one of these under the age of forty. Even then I'd be careful.

If you enjoy reading *Boy's Own*, a young **Peter Pan** can be a pleasant, brief distraction. He has a youthful adventurer's charm. This scores approximately zilch on the Marriage Survival Index. If you do marry him young and by sheer tenacity you're still married to him when his jawline starts to sag, you must be prepared for him to have a twenty-one-gun nervous breakdown.

If you really like Peter Pan, why not wait until he's had his mid-life crisis and then marry him? Once they've got most of that 'Unchain me and let me feel the wind in my hair and the power of my spiffing vroom neeeeow brrrrrmmm little GTI' business out of their system, some of them mature quite nicely. Some of them.

The Pill Popper

There are a lot of these about. Never consider marriage without seeing an inventory of his medicine cabinet first. If it contains more than one remedy for ear-wax, get out while you can. All right, make him an elbow sling, pour him a measure of Calpol and then *get out*!

If a man confides in you about his in-growing eyelash during courtship, imagine what he'll be like after marriage. He will develop multiple conditions – low back pain accompanied by white flecks in his nails and an insatiable craving for liquorice. Or Lassa fever in the Achilles tendon, with rare cardiac complications. And he will discover whole new diseases. He will perplex medical science. If you get pregnant, he will suffer. Varicose veins, carpal tunnel syndrome, Braxton-Hicks contractions – all this after one positive urine test.

Think carefully. Nursing is a tough enough job if you get paid to do it.

Son of Israel

Logically I must now speak about Jewish men since they are usually **one part Peter Pan, three parts Hypochondriac**, stirred but not shaken.

I must first mention their mothers. I know! Writers are always taking cheap shots at Jewish mothers. Normally I'd leave it alone, but on this occasion I have my reasons. It's an old story. Jesus had a Jewish mother. She thought he was God, and the whole thing spread like wildfire. This helps to explain

Jewish men, but not to excuse them. My mother gave me
expectations. I suppose your mother gave you expectations.
Do *we* keep going back to demand a refund?

Jewish men take megalomania to the fourth dimension.
Compulsiveness? Tyranny? Neurosis? Step this way please.
Redeeming features? Certainly. They are often very funny,
especially about themselves. Cunningly they will use this talent
to divert your fury over their latest episode of monumental
obnoxiousness. Also, once you've married him, a Jewish man
will rarely stray. He'll prefer to stay home, in case Killer Ants
invade Mill Hill. You could do worse.

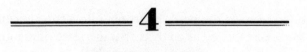

4

In-Laws

When you marry someone you marry their past, their luggage and of course, their family. Even if you never meet any of them, they will always be there. *Even* if you marry the son of a duke and they disinherit him because you are a part-time croupier from a council house in Ilford, and they don't think you're quite suitable, his family will still never go away.

At the start someone else's family can make a welcome change from your own. The kind of uncle that would make you die of shame if he were yours can seem like a bit of a card when he belongs to a family you hope to join. But uncles are small beer. Parents are the thing.

Mothers-in-law have been the butt of so many hundreds of years of propaganda that out of sheer perversity I shall deal with fathers-in-law first.

For girls, fathers-in-law are usually a doddle. If you are a shameless gold-digger, pregnant, or the wrong religion, there may be a little putting down of feet, but kind hearts usually win the day. Men old enough to have marrying sons tend to be completely in favour of young women. You will remind him of his youth. He will show you the medals he got for running when he was in the army, he'll show you the inside of his greenhouse, every last pane of it, and he will be a very good friend to you if you let him, because you are doing him a favour. You are removing, permanently, the fly in his ointment.

Look at it from his point of view. He's worked long and hard. Every penny he's ever had seems to have disappeared down the throat of the lad you intend to marry. He's not been allowed to convert the boy's bedroom into a snug because She Who Must Be Obeyed liked to keep it in a state of readiness for the prodigal's return. But if you marry him, there won't be any return. The lion can reclaim the den, after twenty-six years of waiting, and you can have his son. Gladly.

If you are a man, a father-in-law is a very different kettle of fish. What makes you think you are fit even to *suggest* marrying his daughter? Who says you may even breathe the same air as this flower of womanhood? This girl, make no mistake, is a princess. You might have picked her up on a NALGO picket line. You might have seen what she can do with a Black and Decker, a pile of timber, and a spare Saturday afternoon. But to Daddy she is Shirley Temple. You needn't bother getting your family tree fixed. Don't think that a bespoke suit and an AmEx card will help you either. Whoever you are, you gotta be trash. Stands to reason. Yes, probably even if you are the trainee King of England. I'm sorry, but we may as well face facts. Whatever your credentials, your intentions are dishonourable. You are going to snatch this child from the bosom of her family. You're going to subject her to savage initiation rites, like Late Night Shopping at Asda. Sometimes you'll yell at her. And then there'll be childbirth. *Childbirth!* Another double brandy please, and fetch the angina pills! It is probably fair to say that her Daddy would like to see you undergo major surgery.

But there is good news. When you have been married to his daughter for a few years, his attitude will change. He will think of you as a married man. You will have his sympathy and his understanding. You may have married Shirley Temple, but look how she turned out! The first time your father-in-law winks at you, go take a look in the mirror. See that hang-dog look? Where have you seen it before? Correct. Your father-in-law is now your friend. He just let you into the club.

Women still don't feature much in the Stock Exchange or the Mother of Parliaments. They still don't have anything like the money and influence of men. But in the average Western family they are in the driving seat. I'm not surprised so few women seek the power of public office. They already have so much at home. Power is what mother-in-law jokes are about. Power and fear.

The mother of a grown-up son is in a predicament. On the one hand, as a woman she knows what men are like. On the other, as a mother she wishes to believe that her son is a singular exception. No one else may be willing to see it, but then, no one knows him like she does. Didn't she grow him, give him life, never mind that she can never wear a swimsuit in public again? Didn't she suckle him, wind him, and clean up his little tush? Has she ever stopped? He has his faults, certainly. He threw a paddy once because his sister wouldn't get off the trike. But it was *his* turn. And yes, he does have a habit of clearing his throat when women are speaking, but that's because of his tonsils. The surgeon was a fool. They should have sued. But why search for flaws in someone so patently unblemished?

When your prospective mother-in-law takes her son in her arms and asks, 'How's my best boy?' your heart should sink. Here is a woman better placed than any to tell you that the man you are about to marry grinds his teeth and doesn't wash under his foreskin unless *she* stands over him – and she is cheating on you. I mean, is that Oedipal or what?

With time there may come a mellowing. She will never forgive you that her baby looks as thin as a rail, but she may choose to smile and endure it, for his sake. She'll share some little secrets with you. Treasures, like the first pair of mittens he ever had on a dangly string. And the stick-and-lick Easter card he made her when he was seven.

This is as close as she is likely to allow you. The geniality and the life-raft humour that comes eventually with male in-laws will not happen. A mother-in-law can be a very kind friend when she's not watching her back, but watch her back she must. You are another woman. You may be young, you may not yet know how to bone a leg of lamb, but there you lurk, hungry for power. Given an inch, who can say – you might take all five feet ten of him.

This brings us to the star of the show. The Prima Donna, the Nagger in the Woodpile, the glimpse into the future, the wife's mother. Where would comedy writers be without her?

I once read of a man who jilted his fiancée and ran off with her mother instead. This story was accompanied by the sound of several hundred thousand men throwing up at the very idea.

Whatever the facts, the bride's mother is presumed guilty until proven a hopeless case. She is reputed to have the memory of an elephant, the eye of a hawk, and the cheerful demeanour of a Komodo dragon. Her peevishness has been attributed to the fact that her own physical charms are on the wane. That she is suffering from a type of sexual jealousy and that a son-in-law is the handiest dog to kick.

This is nonsense. Many years ago one man suffered a rough passage at the hands of a shrew on a broomstick. Possibly the cause was pre-menstrual tension. Or maybe the man was just behaving like a proper fool. Whatever the explanation, his terror has passed into folk history. No matter what they may claim, all men are in awe of women. And no wonder! They rule empires on which the sun never sets *and* they know how to make steamed jam roll.

Let me answer a few questions.

Do wives take after their mothers? Not necessarily.

Can I get on the right side of my mother-in-law? Certainly. Everyone has their price. Consult a lion tamer about the psychology of dominance before you make a start.

Exactly how can I achieve connubial bliss and the unstinted blessing of the bride's mother? Roughly speaking, over her dead body.

But seriously. Modern mothers-in-law do not deserve all this calumny. Many of them are handsome, interesting people, too busy and happy to be jealous of younger women or discontented with sons-in-law. If you are unlucky enough to inherit an unreconstructed old niggler you have to be realistic about your chances. Family is family. The best you can do is settle somewhere too far away for impromptu visits. She may involve her daughter in a correspondence course in subversion, and she may vilify you over the telephone every night of the week, but at least she won't be drinking your sherry while she does it.

If she lives just round the corner, or has actually moved in with you, you must fight fire with fire. Demonstrate what happens if you give a dog a bad name. Prove her point at every opportunity. Eventually she will blow a gasket or find fault with something new. That's the good thing about miseries. They're always glad of something different to be miserable about.

Brothers-in-law, sisters-in-law, cousins, aunts, grandparents, these are all peripheral. The world is full of oddballs. His family, her family, haven't cornered the market in undesirables, although it may look that way sometimes.

You will do best if you are not noticeably taller, slimmer, richer or smarter than anyone in the family you are joining. The first time you meet them you can do yourself a lot of good by wearing a few stick-on warts or a pair of Nora Batty stockings. Forget power-dressing. Call a theatrical costumier and see if they have anything your size in the Object of Pity Section. If you have a Double First or anything flash like a Rowing Blue or contacts in the Cabinet Office, play them down. Your moment will come.

Finally, never ask new relatives for a discount or a favour until you've known them at least ten minutes. I know there's a long waiting list for the MCC and this could be your big chance. Just don't blow it, that's all I'm saying.

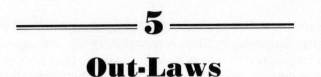

5

Out-Laws

Marrying out is never easy. Families will close ranks faster on this issue than on any other. Your parents brought you up in the hope that you would make a good marriage, and by that they meant you should marry someone of the same colour, faith and politics. If you choose someone from a family or a street they can identify with, or someone whose father belongs to the same golf club as your father, this augurs even better. They don't want to get involved with any fancy religions or bizarre foreign customs, they don't want you selling out, and they don't want to have to explain anything to your Auntie Joyce: 'Don't get me wrong! She's a very lovely girl. It's just that it would have been a lot easier if we could have had the wedding at Sebastopol Street Methodist and then all come back here for a boiled ham salad.'

And wedding arrangements are only the start. When you have been Roman Catholic or Armenian or black or pink all your life, you don't realise how much there is to being it. Without you participating your mind has been filled with neatly filed information on how to think and behave. It has shaped your language, and your expectations. And although love is something that happens between people, not filing cabinets, it doesn't always feel that way. Whoever wrote that song about the world being A Great Big Melting Pot hadn't tried marrying someone from the other side of the tracks.

There are two reasons that mixed marriages cause problems. One is fear of dilution. That the faith won't be so strictly adhered to, or that in the future, family stock will be of a lower quality. Eugenically this is completely up the spout. My understanding is that a good shake-up in the gene pool every so often is entirely beneficial. But try telling that to the duchess.

The second reason mixed marriages get the thumbs down is that old chestnut, human idleness. Cross-cultural marriages require all concerned to make a lot more effort at being adaptable. Instead of turning to the page of that dog-eared script headed Foreigners, Infidels and Class Enemies, we have to accommodate a living, breathing, individual example of one of our prejudices, and possibly admit that he's not so bad after all. A tough assignment this. It's no fluke xenophobia has always been such a hit. The simplest things always are.

Marrying vertically has special significance in Britain. 'Of course,' I said sweepingly to my friend Di, 'in America people aren't obsessed with this class thing.' 'Are you kidding?' she said. 'When Jacqueline Bouvier married that Kennedy trash we felt the tremors down in Baton Rouge!' So maybe I'll recant, a little. But in Britain we have a very long tradition about class barriers. Marrying up is a bitch. So is marrying down, but it's also slightly more fun. Here is an interesting statistic. For every person marrying up, there is a person marrying down.

If you are marrying into the lower classes, the first thing you should know about is the fierceness of their snobbery. It comes of them being an endangered species. Where the middle classes will do virtually anything to improve themselves in the eyes of the world, the so-called working classes will resort to all manner of eee-ba-goom-ery when they're called to man the barricades: 'Toff sighted, two o'clock and closing fast! Get that sauce bottle on the table and clear a path to the outside privy!' This is where the *real* class struggle is going on – in the hearts and minds of the toiling masses. They do know that apart from a few very rich, very idle people, we are all toiling in the same mass – Get up, go to work, worry about the electricity bill, work a bit more, home for a chip butty and the *News at Ten*, if you're lucky get laid and then up in the morning to start again – but as guardians of a tradition, they like to pretend they are toiling in a more picturesque fashion. Stripped to the waist, glistening with sweat. Which is really not necessary when you're loading a Superelectronic 747 Washer Drier.

A family which perceives itself as poor and simple and proud of it will pull all kinds of stunts if it thinks one of its number is going to be gentrified by marriage. Clipping the whippet's dewclaws at table. Talking in strange tongues. Oiling the mangle in the front parlour. But principally they work at dividing the loyalties of the one who intends marrying out, by suggesting at five-minute intervals, that there can be no greater sin, no worse betrayal of kith, kin and those who shed blood on the nightshift at Longbridge, than marrying one of t'Bosses.

Very few families keep this up for long. You shouldn't try to ingratiate yourself. If you are a basically nice person, they'll soon warm to you. Then they'll talk normally, and stop wearing miners' helmets in the house, and you'll discover that they are approximately as kind, cruel, neurotic and funny as any other family you've ever met. The big bonus is that you really can leave the sauce bottle on the table.

Marrying up is different. This is because from where the richer, grander people are looking there's a lot more at stake. Like land, and money.

An important thing to know about aristocracy is that they all know one another. Any one of them, furnished with the flimsiest of biographies, can immediately place another one of them.

'Pleased to meet you, madam.'
'Cressida tells me you're a *Sissil*.'
'Yes your grace.'
'Are you an Exeter *Sissil* or a Salisbury *Sissil*?'
'I'm a Dagenham Cecil, your Highness.'
'Ah . . . Well no matter. You must come and meet my dachshund.'

You can buy books that will help you find your way round the habits of the upper classes, but be careful. Books never tell you everything. And often the bit they left out is the biggest giveaway of all. 'Pass the port to the left,' the book says. But has it mentioned that if you are a girl you shouldn't be passing the port at all? Has it mentioned that when your hostess rises and says, 'Ladies, shall we?' 'No thanks, I had a pee before dinner and I'm dying for a cheroot' is not a permissible answer?

30

What you need is a friend. Someone who knows the score and can be trusted to tell you what it is. Being vague and eccentric may carry you through certain social situations, but you'll still need to know how to eat an artichoke. Sorry, I can't help you there.

Harrods' *Guide to Entertaining* contains an interesting section called 'Creating Atmosphere'. It has pointers on choosing candles and folding napkins into water-lilies, which makes pretty thrilling reading. But I am advised by a veteran that there is truly nothing so electrifying or effective in the creation of atmosphere as the sight of a young and hopeful peasant drinking from his finger bowl.

Until you have found yourself a friend on the inside who will signal discreetly when you are on the brink of another gaffe, here are three vital things to know before marrying up.

1 Always stay on the right side of servants. This means allowing them to do their job. Never clear plates, open doors, or try to deal with your own dirty underwear. And never engage them in idle chit-chat. They know their place, and they expect you to know yours.

2 When eating in fine houses, always make alternative arrangements about food. A few Jaffa Cakes concealed in a hat-box, perhaps? The great and good are invariably thin, have you noticed? After a weekend sharing their meals you'll understand why. Food is served slowly, majestically, and in strict order of social precedence. So the bigger cheese you are, the longer your food has to congeal on the plate before you can get at it. This is just one example of how being grand isn't a lot of fun.

3 *Never* wear diamonds before luncheon.

6

Plighting Your Troth

So you've found yourself this divine partner who's going to make a first-class Old Slipper. Now you have to have a wedding.

Women enjoy weddings far more than men do. Unfortunately a wedding can bring out the worst in a woman – sentimentality, delusions of grandeur, obsessiveness in haberdashery departments, reduced sex drive – and leave a good man bewildered. A man did once say to me, 'I enjoyed every minute of my wedding,' but he was in the divorce courts within two years so I suppose it had been downhill all the way from the moment he left the reception.

I thought I knew you! At least I liked to think I did

For some men the agony begins long before they have to go for fittings at Moss Bros. Some men find it difficult even to tell their mates that a wedding has been arranged. They try to slip it in under Any Other Business. 'I'll raise you a quid. By the way I'm getting married Easter Saturday.' They also like to pretend that aside from the three hours taken up by the ceremony and the reception, life will just go on. They like to pretend that the purpose of a hard-drinking stag night is to lay down ground rules for their leisure time after the wedding. As in 'If I choose to spend our curtain money getting whammed with Tony and Pig Pen, that's the way it'll be sweetheart, take it or leave it.' This of course is a load of nonsense. The true purpose of a stag night is to say farewell to all that.

First Things First

Theoretically, wedding day responsibilities break down as follows. All parties consult about the date, the venue and the degree of lavishness. The bride's father pays for her clothes, the reception, the church flowers, the cars, the invitations, the bride's mother's hat, coat, gloves, handbag, directoire knickers, and Valium, and the cake. The bridegroom pays for his clothes, the ceremony, flowers that are carried or worn, and the ring. What actually happens is that the bride's mother runs the whole show. This is how weddings come to get fixed for the day of the Oaks or the FA cup Final.

An elaborate wedding can take a very long time indeed to arrange. As you wait for the Sugar Rose Specialist to decorate the fifth tier of your wedding cake, you begin to understand the appeal of escaping down a ladder and legging it to Gretna Green. Marriages may be best contemplated at length, but weddings are best effected at short notice.

The fastest methods of getting married are by Common Licence or Superintendent Registrar's Certificate and Licence.

Only one clear day's notice is needed before the licence can be issued. Banns take longer. They have to be read aloud in church on three consecutive Sundays preceding the wedding. If you live in different parishes, they have to be read in both places, and it is only polite for one of you to be present for at least one of the readings. This is when you discover that the *full* name of the person you have loved and known as Bill is actually Nehemiah Reginald William.

Practical advice on arranging a wedding isn't difficult to come by. There are any number of handbooks, with checklists and suggested timetables. In the 1987 edition of one popular guide I was relieved to see a reminder to the bride's mother to send invitations to her servants, a gift suggestion list that included *two* tray cloths (can you still buy tray cloths?) and a prudent word to the bride on the length of her train – more than three feet and we are talking cathedrals. See? There's a lot to think about.

Best Men

The choice of a Best Man is not always an obvious one. You may have a very good friend, who would give you his last Silk Cut, and even lend you his angle-grinder, but is he really the man to make a speech before a hundred and fifty petalled hats? Can he speak at all beyond simple reflexes like, 'Here we go, here we go, here we go!' And can he be expected to understand that the one about the Pope and the man with a condom on his nose would be better saved for a more private moment?

Best friends may stop being best friends if you burden them with the responsibility of looking after the ring, kissing girls dressed in Clearasil and peach satin, *and* being charming to your in-laws. If your bride has a brother, choose him. Then, if he blows it, you'll qualify for sympathy that your generous trust in a member of *her* family has been abused. In fact you'll come up generally smelling of roses.

Zero Hour

There are certain features that are common to all marriage ceremonies whatever the denomination. One is that the groom arrives before the bride. How he arrives is irrelevant. A Number 11 bus, even a push-bike will do. As long as the Best Man remembers about the bike-clips before the bride's mother arrives. It is not done to squeeze past the bridal procession with a tub of Polyfilla, wheezing, 'You should have seen the queues in Texas!'

Something else. Ceremonial often calls for behaviour that doesn't come naturally. Dignified kneeling. Walking with a measured tread. You could do worse than close the curtains and practise a little.

Vows are not difficult to make. Royals only fluff them because it makes good TV. There is always someone there to prompt you, even through the shortest bits. The tough part of vows is keeping them.

Wedding rings only get lost in the movies. This could be a terrific idea for the next Royal wedding. A commercial break while someone of noble birth turns out his pockets. Real people don't lose rings.

After the marriage registers have been signed, a little jollity is allowed to break out. It's a natural release from the nervous tension of the ceremony. Kissing is even permitted provided it is kept within bounds. However pent up you may be feeling, this is not the moment to have your tongue inside anyone's ear.

On Parade

The purpose of a wedding reception is to prove to the world that your stag night has achieved its goal and you are now under control in public. There is no need to concern yourself with guest lists, or which fork to use first. All this will be taken

35

care of by your elders and betters. They will have lists, blueprints, lists of lists, and the ultimate precaution of a hired double who can stand in for you if you are overtaken by drink or regret. In return you are expected to smile.

There is a lot to be said for just going to the pub, or having one of those standing buffets where everyone drops flaky pastry down their waistcoat. As soon as you decide to seat people you run the risk of putting guests on a war footing with each other and with you. A seating plan is a masterpiece of diplomatic endeavour. Bridesmaids take precedence over grandparents, aunts take precedence over the Pontypool Front Row, and anyone who has flown in from Tasmania specially for the occasion takes precedence over everyone else.

With some families you can follow protocol to the letter and still end up needing a UN peace-keeping force. If you get too many tantrums, you can always threaten to cancel the banqueting suite and order two hundred Quarterpounders with Cheese To Go.

Pray Silence

A wedding is one of those occasions when people get asked to say a few words. The strange thing is, they never do. They go on and on. Anyone would think they were accepting a BAFTA award.

First, someone proposes the health of the bride and groom. This can be a real Dickie Attenborough marathon. Ideally you want an old family friend who has the wit to stop before he is interrupted by the sound of snoring. What you will probably get is someone who begins his slow wind-up with '. . . and it gives me great pleasure to propose this toast, remembering as I do young Rosemary, dressed only in a vest, singing "Animal Crackers in My Soup". It seems like only yesterday, though in fact it must be all of six months ago. And talking of soup reminds me of another story . . .'

When this ends, the bridegroom replies. As long as he includes the phrases 'My wife and I', 'Many, many, many thanks' and anything that uses the words *lovely, wonderful* and *beautiful,* all will be well. *Mega* and *brill* are not recommended, and without being a smart arse you should pad things out a little so it *feels* like a speech. Saying, 'Triff to see you all and thanks a bunch for the prezzies,' isn't quite enough.

At the end of his speech, the bridegroom toasts the bridesmaids.

Bridesmaids don't reply. They are supposed to be silent and decorative. The Best Man replies for them. Remember what I said about the Best Man? Your Best Man may have known you since your first day at school. He may remember when you both caught crabs, and when you nearly married Elaine who was a right little goer. But you won't want him to say so. It will be sufficient for him to say, 'On behalf of Olive and Beryl, the lovely bridesmaids, thank you for your good wishes. May I now ask you all to join with me in drinking the health of the parents of the bride and groom.' Cut. It's a wrap.

Reading out the telegrams when people are starting to need the bathroom is a mean thing to do. Actually, they're not called telegrams any more, but whatever they're called, no one ever sent a witty one. Off the cuff, Groucho Marx came up with 'Marriage is a wonderful institution, but who wants to live in an institution!' but if he had had to fill in a British Telecom form it would have turned out more like 'May all your troubles be little ones. From Mr Wiggitt and all in Menswear at the Royston Co-Op.'

After the speeches you have to cut the cake. Here is another important tip from *Wedding Etiquette 1987* – cutting with your husband's sword will be much easier if an incision has been made beforehand and lightly iced over. So now you know.

Wedding cake is the last straw. Solemn vows, prayers for divine assistance, melon, stringy roast chicken, strangers thumping you between the shoulder-blades, photographs of it all with PROOF written across them – this is all bad enough, without cake you can only eat if you don't mind getting currants between your front teeth. You're not really meant to eat it. I think it's just a symbol. It symbolises that once you're married you can't have your cake *or* eat it. Or maybe it's supposed to be lucky. Lucky cake. I'll tell you what is lucky – a chimney sweep. Also, a spider, a toad or a black cat. If you see any of those on the way to your wedding the signs are good. A funeral, or a pig, things don't look so hot. This is the trouble with omens. A girl could clean up on the way to the church – sweeps, cats, the whole bit – but if she meets a pig on the chancel steps she's going to need more than a bit of luck.

7

Close Quarters

In old movies, when there was a wedding, there was always a scene that fascinated me. It came after the champagne and the jock-talk between the friends of the groom. The bride changed into a nipped-waist costume with a little matching hat, and her mother took her into a bedroom for A Few Words. Before I'd been married myself I imagined that what Mother had to say went something like this:

'Celia, darling . . . Now you're a wife, there is something I have to tell you. There's a thing men do. All men do it, even nice men like Bertie, and as his wife it is your duty to allow it. Be brave, my darling! If it's terribly horrid, think of something nice. Think of your lovely silver-plate teapot, or your Royal Worcester cake-stand. If you do that, you'll find that it won't seem to go on for so long. And you must remember, Bertie can't help it. Heavens, it's probably as horrid for him as it is for you, and he'll stop doing it as soon as he possibly can. I'm so glad we chose lilac for your blouse. You look divine . . .'

I was wrong. I realised this within twenty-four hours of living with a man. Mothers don't take their daughters into bedrooms to advise them to sing 'Pollywollydoodle' during sexual congress. They do it to warn them about the other sorts of intimacy.

'Celia, there's something you should know about men. They do press-ups before breakfast, get axle grease on the towels, and put everything in the laundry basket inside out. What's more, they leave the lavatory seat up, cut their toenails in bed, and they fart, anywhere, everywhere, and at all times.'

And then I wondered, when did fathers have a few words with their sons? I mean, fair's fair. You can't have brides genned up on the loathsome traits of men, if bridegrooms aren't forewarned that women shave their legs with men's razors, never dip for oil, and hardly ever do *anything* without a generous application of handcream and a pair of rubber gloves.

This is the stuff of married life. Close encounters with bristles in the sink and dripping pantihose.

It's really a question of expectations. Clearly, if all you know of your partner is what you've seen over dinner at the Connaught and the occasional rubber of whist, marriage is going to be a rude awakening. Living together before marriage avoids this big shock. It accustoms you to another person's foul habits before you make a legal commitment. It's a sensible, modern idea, which unfortunately destroys the special pioneer excitement of a journey into the unknown. You can't have it both ways.

What you can do is get in perspective the awfulness of the bed you have to lie in. There you are, a paragon of reason and sobriety, joined in wedlock with a character from *Caligula*. Where do you start? You start by recognising three categories of bad habits. Those that are of an involuntary nature, those related to normal bodily functions, and those connected with domestic practicalities. There will always be some overlap, but this three-way split at least helps the mind cope with the enormity of the problem.

We can dispose of **Involuntary Habits** swiftly and unsatisfactorily. There is absolutely nothing you can do about them. Except make a list of them:

Teeth grinding. Ear waggling. All facial tics. Nail biting. Table drumming. Whistling. Whistling through the teeth. Whistling something dead obvious from *La Bohème*.

Feeling any better?

If you are married to a table-drumming teeth-whistler, you have my sympathy. But the question is, what's your vice?

Maybe you should ask someone. Someone who's been wanting to tell you for years that the way you keep playing with your bi-focals is driving them demented. There are probably people out there in therapy because of you and your specs.

Never think you're going to cure anyone of habits like this. Never think, 'I'll marry Gordon. But the first thing I'm going to do when we get back from Jersey is get that humming seen to!' If Gordon hums, Gordon will continue to hum. Humming is an inoperable condition. So is knuckle-cracking. And sniffing.

Snoring is different. It is a mysterious thing. Men snore more than women. As they're asleep when they're doing it, it's hard to see that there's anything you can do about it except buy ear-plugs. But it is now possible to buy a Snore Corrective. I don't know how it works, but I'm told it is humane and costs only a few pounds. If you're living with a bad case, anything is worth a try. Of course, any widow will tell you that snoring is the sweetest sound this side of heaven.

41

Unnecessary Sharing of Bodily Functions

This area is pretty well monopolised by men. If it seems like I'm picking on the chaps *again*, just wait till we talk about Abuse of the Vacuum Cleaner.

Men generally have a very straightforward attitude to the way their bodies work. If it itches, they scratch. What goes up must come down, what goes down will sometimes come up, and the only thing to do with wind is release it into the atmosphere. Noses, teeth and fingernails are for picking. Why else would the Lord have given us forefingers and Hygienol Interdental Gunge Removers? And then there are navel fluff, snuggles between the toes, early morning eye-crud, and the consequences of a bad cold. Oh yes, and armpits. Nearly forgot the armpits.

Now I do not mean to suggest that women don't pick their noses, belch, or sniff their armpits. I don't think I'm betraying any confidences when I tell you that they do all of those and more. The difference between men and women is that the things women try to do privately, men prefer to do on the stage of the London Palladium.

Lest this whole chapter become unreadable through the miasma of bodily secretions, I intend to take one odious habit and deal with that in depth. This will then stand as an example, and as a symbol.

I have chosen a phenomenon that transcends all barriers of class, race and creed. If women cannot unite in the cause of World Peace, they can unite in their suffering of this invidious practice. Bishops do it. Honourable Members do it. Nobility, Privy Councillors, brain surgeons. Lamp-lighters do it, but not as much as they used to. Hill shepherds do it, and so do deep-sea fishermen, but at least they do some of it in the great outdoors. Gandhi did it in his *ashram*. Wellington did it in his tent. And so did Napoleon. Queen Victoria did it, but Prince Albert did it a lot more. They farted, what else? Show me a man and I will show you a woman with her hand covering her nose. Farting, rip-snorting, blowing off, cutting the cheese, dropping one, guffing, whiffing, powering the National Grid, we could go on all night. Okay, everyone makes gas. It's the manner of passing it that is under scrutiny here.

Men do it noisily. *Con gusto.* Some of them have baffle-plates fitted to improve the bass tones. They choreograph it. When seated they raise one cheek. When standing they raise one leg, and in the bath they count the bubbles. Above all else, they savour the moment. 'Ah,' they say, 'this is a good one. Mainly port and stilton at a guess.' This is the voice of pride. Then there is the voice of the misunderstood: 'Myra, don't give me that prune-faced look! If you feed me onions three nights running, what do you expect, Attar of Roses? Actually, there is a slightly floral undernote in there.' Pride sneaking in again at the end.

As if all this is not enough, men signal to each other that they've just done it. It is acceptable behaviour. It's not like insider-dealing, or ripping the felt on a chap's billiard table. Girls, don't be upset that you can't sit in the Members' Library at the Carlton Club. You wouldn't want to, believe me! They fan the air and grimace with mock disgust. 'Without a word of a lie,' they say, over a lunch of Scotch eggs and draught Guinness, 'I let one slip last night that should have been covered in foam and dealt with by the Royal Engineers.' 'Good was it?' enquires his admiring audience. 'Good? I'm not one for blowing my own trumpet but put it this way, Jean's had to go to Switzerland for her lungs!' This is the human equivalent of the lamp-post marking done by dogs. Territory, *again.*

If you need convincing, there is a final, familiar scenario that demonstrates perfectly how farting is a clever way of defining personal space.

It is late. Ted is in bed reading *Practical Gardening*, and Doreen is slapping on the Oil of Ulay. The bathroom isn't at the end of the garden, it is just across the landing. Nor is Ted disabled in any way. He has the use of his legs. He has a dressing-gown and a pair of Bully Bull's Eye slippers. If he needed to fart, you'd think, wouldn't you, that he'd get up and do it before Lights Out? But he waits until Doreen is in bed, comfortable, and toying with the choice of a couple of rows of knitting or orgiastic sex, and *then* he does it. If they've been married more than a week, he makes a joke of it. 'Call out the Civil Defence!' he quips. 'Evacuate all children and sick animals!' And if he's a twenty-two carat sadist, he pulls the duvet over their heads and holds it down tight.

Under analysis he would probably say that he was defending his sexual territory. That he was deterring any red-blooded interloper from leaping between the sheets and having his way with Doreen's knitting. Doreen would say he was just bad-mannered.

This brings us to the other big category of offences against the person – **Domestic**.

Stacking the plates while people are still eating, hot-washing Barbour jackets, riding the clutch, putting sugar in Pouilly Fumé, keeping cups of chicken stock in the fridge and never using them, leaving the lavatory seat down, and vacuuming while Match of the Day is in Progress. Frankly girls, this is not good enough. But then neither is offering to do the washing-up but leaving the cheese-grater and the scrambled-egg pan for someone else, failing to replace an empty toilet roll, or using a soufflé dish to mix fungicidal wallpaper paste. This problem is as long as it's wide.

Everyone has sensible reasons for doing what they do. If the rest of the world is wrong-footed, is it your fault? Unless both partners in a marriage are easy-going in the extreme, there has to be some making of allowances and turning of blind eyes.

In our marriage we have agreed certain trade-offs. I will not leave dishes on the draining-board all day, if he will not wipe the floor with the dishcloth. He will not have six aerosol cans of deodorant running concurrently, all in different states of emptiness, if I quit splashing hair dye on the shower curtain. And he'll stop setting fire to the kitchen, if I will. See? With a little maturity and effort these things can be resolved.

Although, what *do* you do with a woman who creases newspapers and shuffles the pages so you can't find the First Class Averages? Even patient men have their limits.

Offences Against The Married Person Act 1988

Before an individual can be convicted of a crime it is necessary to prove that his conduct has caused a certain state of affairs, and that his conduct was accompanied by a prescribed state of mind. *Both* elements must be proved beyond reasonable doubt. Or, as my Auntie Peggy always said, *actus non facit reum nisi mens sit rea.*

Lighting a Stinking Pipe:
By Section 43 this is punishable with a two-month suspension from St Bruno (on indictment) or by Section 44, on summary conviction, with one month's hard labour at the sink or a fine not exceeding a bottle of scent and a box of Milk Tray. Since this is not a crime of specific intent, drunkenness is no defence.

Going Equipped with a Vacuum Cleaner:
s.13(4) applies to use of a vacuum cleaner to resist kissing a husband with two days' beard growth, possession of a crevice tool with intent, and discharging a vacuum cleaner in a built-up area, without lawful authority, during the transmission of the World Snooker Championship semi-final.

It does not include vacuum cleaners adapted or intended for incapacitating a person, or unlawful restraint with an upholstery nozzle.

Convicted persons are liable to three weeks' major building works without recourse to a carpet sweeper, or a fine not exceeding a bottle of single malt or a ticket for the Lord's Test.

8

Fixtures and Fittings

When a man and a woman first set up home together there is a lot more to be settled than the colour of the washing-up bowl.

You can meet someone at a party, see them again for a dinner or two, walk hand in hand along a deserted winter beach, truly believing you have found perfection. And then discover that perfection likes to sleep between tangerine nylon sheets, and keep his tobacco in a hollowed elephant's foot. The tempestuous beauty who's been reading you Shelley and running barefoot through your fantasies, has a five-foot Roland Rat in her sitting room and Kate Greenaway stickers on her fridge door.

The moment you agree to marry someone, you find out they're colour blind and inseparable from nasty things you never dreamed they were capable of owning. Somehow you have to whittle away at each other's ugly possessions, and eventually you have to agree on how to feather a whole nest.

From the start I must leave aside those who are marrying or married to interior designers. I should imagine your best plan might be to go away for a year or two until everything is complete. Interior designers are trained to make foolish and expensive decisions all alone, so you won't be missed.

Quite often, amongst ordinary ignorant people who wouldn't know a kelim from a hole in the head, there emerges one partner who is happy to soldier on and do a whole house single-handed, and one who is happy to let them. A partnership of this kind has the makings of domestic bliss.

So have the ones between two people who never notice

anything about their environment. Couples like that can move into a cold-water flat and never change a thing. They save pounds on paint and parlour palms.

But the relationships that founder in soft-furnishing departments are the ones between people with strongly held views on the science of colour:

'I *do* love you Norma! I just get this really adverse karma from primrose yellow!'

Or, 'Lionel, we're not buying it. It's exactly the colour of cat shit. Hang on, though. Maybe you're on to something here. I'm beginning to see where you're coming from. Okay, agreed, we do everything in Cat Shit.'

I've just finished looking at several dozen books on interior design. Your typical bachelor, it seems, chooses bottle-green gloss paint, dark oak and leather. Solid, permanent-looking stuff that will last for years, because there is absolutely nothing wrong with being a bachelor. Spinsters, on the other hand, are merely wives-in-waiting. So they choose pastels, sheers, and wipeable white furniture that collapses after six months.

This is very odd. Because nearly every young, single person I've ever known had paper lamp-shades, cheap posters papered over the cracks, and quite a lot of cast-offs from anyone over the age of forty who was generous enough to give. We grow up with our parents' mish-mash, leave home and move down-market to our own single version, and in the fulness of time try to marry our personal chaos to someone else's. We study shade cards, play around with sheets of graph paper and scale models, and still end up with curtains that scream at the rugs. There is something rather comforting about this reality. If you are an interesting enough person ever to be the subject of an in-depth article by *Ideal Home*, you will need proper professional advice. If you are merely mortal, here are some things you should know about creating a beautiful home.

1 As a couple, are you **Improvers** or **Restorers**? Improvers cover bad ceilings with polystyrene tiles. Restorers rip them off and enjoy the natural charm of precarious plaster. Still not sure? Restorers love black-leaded grates in bedrooms, baths with claw feet, and plaster mouldings. Improvers don't. Improvers like to get a nice big piece of hardboard and cover all that Edwardian junk up. An Improver should never marry a Restorer. Obviously. Marriage is supposed to be a largely pleasant experience, not a pitched battle with chipboard and shavehooks.

2 Are you essentially **Urban, Rural** or **Suburban People**? This may sound too basic to be worth answering, but you would be surprised how many people buy terraced houses in Stoke Newington and then decide they want to keep goats. Keep goats, breed them, milk them, and make their own cheese! You really cannot go against the grain in this way. I know those people did it in 'The Good Life', but that was television. If you live in a city street you must go and buy your cheese from a shop, and if you can't control your urge to make cheese, you must buy a place with an airy dairy out the back. Furthermore, if you are so much a townie that you can't get to sleep without police sirens, you shouldn't marry any closet dairy farmer who might suddenly ask you to move to a barn in Suffolk. Not even for love.

This is why suburbia is such a good bet. In the suburbs you can be whoever you want to be. Put a peacock on your lawn and pretend you're nobility. Or plough it all up and never have to buy another potato. Suburbia gets a regular knocking from the town lobby and the fresh air brigade, but the people who live there couldn't give a damn. Consider all those rows of identical houses. Builders can't put them up fast enough. Decent folk queue to buy them. They can't all be wrong. Could this be the life for you?

If you think it might be, assemble the following basic equipment: a barometer; a set of sundae glasses; a pouffe; a gateau platter; a patio set; a patio set weatherproof cover; and a chiming door-bell. Please note, *no gnomes*. People who consider themselves above suburbia sneer about garden gnomes, but that just goes to show how little these smart alecs know. Gnomes are actually something of a rarity. I'd organise a bit of crazy paving, though, if I were you.

3 **The Correct Way to Hang Wallpaper**. Clean and prepare all surfaces. Remove from the room as much furniture as you can. Cover what remains with dustsheets and then pay two lads called Den and Den's brother to get on with it while you go to Brighton for the weekend. Remember, when choosing a paper, to allow for pattern repeats in your measurements, to allow for the encroaching effect of four walls of red and gold Taj Mahal flock, and to allow for something that looked perfect in the sample book to look nauseatingly insistent when Den and his brother have

stuck it all over your bedroom. I always think it's hard to beat white emulsion.

4 Whadda ya want, **a work of art or somewhere to hang your coat**? These are dangerous times. Fifty years ago, if you got married and you wanted a wardrobe, you saved sixpences in a jar until you could afford to go to the Co-Op and get one. The temptation now is to go to a DIY store and pretend that making your own *fitted* wardrobes is as easy as boiling an egg. A lot of couples get so desperate for hanging space that they call each other's bluff.

'If we go and pick up the wood first thing on Saturday, we could be finished by Sunday afternoon.'

'Okay' she says, but what she's thinking is, 'Am I wise to allow this?'

'Oh no!' he thinks, 'She's agreed to it! Why did she do that! She knows I can't saw straight. Can't back out now. I just have to hope they don't have the right size doors in stock.'

But they do have the doors, and you buy them. Also a new saw, a snazzy ten-piece screwdriver and a big tin of Band-Aid.

And are you finished by Sunday afternoon? Of course not. Sunday afternoon you have some holes in the wall, a lot of brave talk about battening, and real problems.

'Hold it up and keep it still, Sandra! For Chrissakes keep it still!'

'My arms are hurting.'

'*My* arms are hurting. Am *I* bellyaching about it? Now slide it along a bit until it slots in. A bit further! *Slide* it, don't wave it around! Just a shade more. Sandra! I said a *shade*! Well that's it. You waved when you should have slid. That's the whole wardrobe ruined!'

'Songs of Praise' comes on and all you have to show for your weekend is a stack of firewood. Better really to have been honest from the beginning. Better to hang your clothes from the picture rail and live happily ever after.

5 Is it true that you can create a lily pond, a croquet lawn and an Elizabethan herb garden in one Saturday afternoon?
No.

6 And if you were to be cast away in a pre-war semi for the next thirty years, what, apart from the Bible, the Complete Works of Shakespeare, and a Swiss Army knife, would you find most useful to have with you?
A big tub of jollop for bunging up holes; the longest extension cable known to man; and a case of Scotch, delivered weekly.

Living space is best chopped up into self-sealing units unless you are totally at one with your partner. A great big loft, with a futon and a couple of bead curtains, is no way to live if you like to slip away occasionally for a crafty fag. We all need escape routes from the voice of Harry Carpenter and the sight of women in heated curlers. And we all need somewhere to keep the things we love. This is the killer. Never mind whether the couch matches the curtains – the question is, where are you going to hide the junk? You have to stick it some place, otherwise *Ideal Home* will never call you up to make that appointment.

You need somewhere for shrimping nets and ice-axes. Somewhere for collections of *Eagle* comics not quite old enough to be of any value, for mildewed tents, and pranged Teasmade machines. Ideally you want a room off the beaten track, so you don't have to include it when you do the guided tour. 'Love the pine-clad dinette, Jeff. What's in here?' Do you really want people to know you own two Flab-Blasters and a Dansette?

Some confident types hang all their rubbish from butcher's hooks and manage to make it look fabulous. You can't see their ceilings for flat irons and gin traps, all stylishly displayed and easily to hand. But if you're that kind of person, you won't be reading this. The kind of people who read this fill lofts and

52

cupboards and the spaces under beds, and they still need a drawer for the smaller pieces of flotsam and jetsam. A drawer full of closure wires for dustbin sacks, pens that don't write, and a bit of plastic from a window-cleaning gadget that you let someone borrow and never got back. It is arguable whether any marriage is complete without **A Drawer**.

Gadgets can be problematical even before they end up borrowed or hurled into the cupboard with the tent and the comics. Some people see the point of any gadget immediately. Others still need convincing that the wheel will catch on. The trouble is, gadget-freaks usually marry Luddites. It seems to be part of some divine plan to make marriage even more of a joy-ride.

People who love gadgets can't help it. It's in the blood. Prevention is difficult, cure is impossible. You might as well spit into the wind. It is easier for dyed-in-the-wool nostalgists to overcome technophobia than it is to ask their partner to live without a food processor.

In a sense, gadgets can reduce life to a state of exquisite simplicity. Couples used to need an incredible quantity of hardware before they could even contemplate running a home. They used to need a fish kettle, and an enamelware slop pail. They daren't move without first obtaining a larding needle, a jelly bag and a paste jagger. (No, sorry, I don't know what you do with a paste jagger either.) Then, just when they thought they were in the clear to light the gas and have their first brew up, that terrible moment of realisation: 'We forgot to buy any housemaids' cloths!' What a long way we've come. Now, as long as you have a sharp knife, a galvanised bucket, and a fourteen-day remote control VCR with Still Frame Facility, you have the ingredients of a cosy night in.

Never forget, being asked to live with a tournament-sized snooker table is not grounds for divorce. Nor is a water-bed with a slow puncture. Eclecticism, that's the secret. You've got to think eclectic!

9

Worldly Goods

In every marriage there is a division of labour. One of you cleans the rotten leaves out of the guttering, one of you arranges the flowers; one of you has the delinquent children, and one of you balances the books. Commonly accounts were done by husbands, because women combined with large sums of money were not thought to be a very good idea. Today it is as likely to be the wife as it is the husband, and for every wife who works out the budget and pays the bills, there are a dozen more who would do it, and could do it, if only they had enough information to work with. These are the wives who don't know what their husband makes in a year.

There are plenty of women who couldn't care less. As long as they have enough to pay at the supermarket every Friday, and a new frock twice a year, they are happy. Unwaged themselves, they prefer to be childishly innocent about salaries and taxes. Which is all very well as long as the man who takes care of the money is alive and well. But most wives outlive their husbands. Sooner or later they do have to think about money, and there are few sadder sights than a grieving woman, in her fifties or sixties, trying to understand a tax return for the first time in her life.

Most women know what their husband earns. At least, they think they do. If a husband really wants to conceal some of his income from his wife he can do it. At the moment this option is not open to a woman. For Income Tax purposes *her* income is deemed to be part of *his* income. It is declared on *his* tax return. She can elect for her earnings to be separately assessed for tax, or even taxed separately, but those earnings must still be declared on her husband's tax form. Margaret Thatcher may be First Lord of the Treasury, but for now she has to get Denis to put her on his form.

In 1990 this will change. A wife will then be able to declare her earnings on her own tax form. Any unearned income she receives will be treated as hers for the purposes of Income Tax, instead of being aggregated with her husband's income, and for the first time in the history of tax law she will be as entitled as her husband to whatever privacy in her financial affairs *she* wants.

In a perfect marriage, tendencies to squander and to cheesepare are balanced. This means that he can buy twelve-year-old malt whisky, as long as he's willing to make do with the socks he's had since he was a Junior Sea Scout, and she can buy hand-made Belgian chocolates, because she economised and made herself a winter coat from a pre-war candlewick bedspread. This achieves a kind of equilibrium whereby, at the end of the month, there is enough left in the kitty to pay the bills.

It hardly ever turns out that way. Either you are a committed spendthrift, or you are not. If you are, or more to the point, if you are married to someone who is, it is useful to know the exact path the disease has taken.

The easiest type to deal with is the **Barefaced Spender**. With these people there is never any pretence at economy. The sight of piles of bank notes does nothing for them. They see bank notes as an intermediate nuisance in the exciting process of acquiring lovely, desirable things and giving them away, to themselves or to other people.

The most effective course of action with a Barefaced Spender is to snap all his credit cards in half, and keep him away from shops, markets, bars, restaurants and booking offices. Saturday afternoons they should be grounded. Remove all mail order catalogues from the room, empty their pockets of Pizza-by-Phone menus, and instruct Ladbrokes that they are not to accept a telephone bet under any circumstances. Half measures will get you nowhere. Depending on your own disposition one of their best/worst habits is that they never buy anything useful or essential. The house just fills up with delightful luxury goods, and choleric letters from the bank.

'Bernard, you went out for Rawlplugs and a litre of milk.'
'I *knew* I'd gone out for something.'
'What's in the bag, Bernard?'
'I bumped into George outside the post office.'
'The bag, Bernard. What's in the bag.'
'Nothing much. A Rolex Oyster, and a nice little bin-end from Tipplers. I'll just go back for the milk . . .'

Some apparent Barefaced Spenders are impostors. Usually these are men. They work at a reputation for extravagance so that they will never be asked to do the shopping. It is a financial variant of Bungler's Law of Feigned Stupidity (*q.v.* in 'Keeping the Home Fires Burning'). It doesn't take a lot of brains to work out that if the first time you're sent to Presto you return with smoked salmon and no Vim, you won't get sent again. Newly-married women should be especially vigilant for this little ruse.

Then there is the **Concealed Spendthrift**. Concealed, because they hardly ever pay the full price for anything. They buy second-hand, and in sales, and it's difficult to appreciate how much they're costing you because they always seem to be saving you so much. My experience is that they are predominantly women. Having said that, the first example that springs to mind is a man.

He began as so many of us do, newly-wed and on his beam end. Every week he read the small For Sale ads in the local paper, and his favourite reading was the Under-a-Fiver column. (I suppose by now it's called Under-a-Tenner.) In the first year of his marriage he bought more fridges for £4.99 than you can imagine. They all needed new motors. New enamel, new door seals. If he had had the technology to take them all to pieces and use the best bit from each one, he still couldn't have frozen himself a lolly. Week after week I heard him say, 'We'll be quids in. Quids!' It is the kind of addiction that drags people down very fast.

Soon he was buying carpets that didn't fit, and beat-up old chairs no one could sit in. His wife started drinking tonic wine. He meant well. He had a little nest and he wanted to feather it. Who can blame him? But the next stage was even more grave. He started buying things that even he couldn't pretend were useful. He bought a fireguard. They had radiators in every room. And then, he bought a fibreglass canoe. With two holes in it. He didn't canoe, she didn't canoe. They didn't even live by the side of a lake where they could hire it out at profit. Worse still, they had nowhere to put it. They had been careful to keep the early years of their marriage uncluttered by animals and children and suddenly they were sharing a small flat with a useless boat. Mind you, what a saving! This was when his wife kicked the tonic wine, cancelled the newspapers, and took a tough line. Quite right too.

But I was saying, this is usually a female speciality. I know dozens of women who buy things in sales and the things are not exactly what they wanted, but there was such a killing to be made. In particular they seem drawn to furnishing fabrics. They spend hours carefully planning to have grey chintz with a scarlet lining to pick up the detail colour on the couch, and then they come home with something yellow printed with liquorice allsorts. Because 'they were giving it away.' Of course they were.

This is a very difficult trait to get the better of. After all, their intentions are so decent. They are genuinely trying to save both of you money. I think the kindest thing is to make them a small allowance. Consider it dead money. All but the most miserly of us waste money on something, so if you are married to someone who gets lit up over fag ends of curtain material, why not write it off with those magazines you never read cover to cover, and call it Fun Money?

Tight-wads need Fun Money too. Once every five years they like to get it out of the bank and look at it.

A fairly surprising fact about misers is that they do marry. To me this is contradictory behaviour, marriage being a giving, sharing institution, but I suppose there are savings to be made. Light bulbs, roof repairs, that kind of thing.

The meanest person I ever knew was a man, and a bachelor. He had a pile in the bank, but he was also attracted to the concept of marriage. It was never going to happen. I'll tell you why. In the interests of frugality he had only one jacket. He made further economies by never taking it to the dry cleaners. This man, no kidding, was *stinking* rich. Of course, even that need not have stood in his way. If body odour was a serious impediment to marriage the whole tradition would have died out with chain-mail and Trial by Ordeal. No, the reason this fetid charmer would never marry was that the first question he ever asked any woman was 'How much do you have on deposit?' And if she was stupid enough to tell him, he wanted to know more. 'Is it in Preferential High Yield or Easy Access?' He got what he deserved.

Married misers live in a permanent state of conflict. They have vowed publicly to divvy out. How can they? How can they trust another fickle human being to watch every penny? If you have married a meanie, there are things you should know. First, they are not mean, they are careful. Second, they talk an awful lot of sense. They work hard for their money, you work hard for yours, so why fritter it? All it takes is a little foresight here, a little belt-tightening there, and savings can be made. These people are the backbone of England. The trouble is, when they have made their small but worthwhile savings, what have they got? A bit more money. And what do they do with it? They bank it, so it can keep the other bits warm. Do they ever blow it on pleasure, or give it away? No. Why? Because there isn't really anything they want to possess or to do. Except take it with them.

Meanies do not intend to be defeated by eyes of needles. They are going to have a money belt sewn into their shroud. Because, who knows, across the Vale of Tears there may be attractive investments to be made.

I knew a meanie. What that girl couldn't do with a quarter of mince and three turnips wasn't worth a mention. She would help herself to cream with my freshly-ground Blue Mountain coffee and ask, 'How much are you paying for butter?' Some people enjoy a game of squash, some like to grow roses. She got her kicks baiting reckless squanderers. She knew perfectly well I couldn't tell her what I was paying for butter. To me, butter was just one of those things. If we needed it, I bought it. If my purse was empty, we ate our bread dry. I offer this by way of explanation, not excuse. I may be right, I may be wrong. Christine was certain I was wrong, but actually she had only steered the conversation round to the price of butter so she could tell me how cheap she was getting hers.

She moved away and we lost touch. Phone calls cost, and as she had always reminded me, you have nothing to show for them.

For a long time I couldn't work out why I found this

providential streak so deeply unattractive. Then the daylight dawned. These people are only mean with their own money. If someone else is willing to cough up, they are the first to the bar. This must mean that if one Tight-Wad marries another they will be at a permanent standstill on expenditure. The only place they will ever go is to bed early to save fuel. But if, as is more likely, one of you is normal and one of you is mean, the answer is to reduce those long sulky evenings going over the ledger books by means of a little deceit. I'm sorry. I know it doesn't sound very nice. But if you are married to someone who rations matches, scrupulous honesty and a joint account can be a fast route to the divorce courts. You must have some money, even if it is only a very little indeed, that only you know about. Anywhere will do. An old shoe box, an old Swiss bank account.

As a matter of fact I think this is a good idea whoever you're married to. We all need privacy, and we all need to know that from time to time we can spend without asking permission. I mean, if your partner reads the cheque stubs how else are you going to be able to buy yourself a pair of Janet Reger knickers for his birthday?

10

Keeping the Home Fires Burning

Housework is no small matter. It takes 1000 hours a year to maintain two adults in hygiene and comfort. And I'm not talking about the kind of people who have white chair-covers and dinner parties for ten every week. I'm talking about normal people. Add children – say, a three-year-old, and a babe in arms who does nothing but sleep, feed and require a complete change of clothes every two hours, and you can double that figure. Two thousand hours a year! Without reward. You never make progress with a dishcloth. You have to keep wiping just to stand still.

Some couples argue about housework, but not as many as I would have expected. And most disputes seem to be settled by the woman getting on with it, crevice tool in hand, muttering darkly. Not good enough really, is it?

How To Become A House Husband

This will not be as easy as you might think. First, you must prepare yourself for the scale of housework. If you have never done it, full-time and with sole responsibility, you will do well to remember the iceberg phenomenon. Second, women, even bitterly complaining women, are ridiculously obstructive to the learning process. A woman might take ten minutes ensuring she has properly understood a marmalade recipe, but if a man takes thirty seconds to work out how the steam nozzle works on the iron, she will be there at his side saying, 'Move over. I'll do it myself!' Women often want their bread buttered both sides, and this is a fine example. 'Help me, help me!' she cries. 'But help me *exactly* the way I tell you.'

I am not going to dwell on technical detail. Here are a few important things you should know:

1 Housework is repetitious, tedious and physically sapping, but it isn't difficult. Women have shrouded it in protectionist mystique. Lawyers do the same thing. Don't buy it. If someone as untutored and unwilling as I am can run a house for fifteen years without anyone getting typhus or crawling hungry and naked into the market place, *anyone* can do it. Trust me.

2 Much housework is unnecessary. I know women who iron towels. Can you believe that! Some women dust *every day of their lives*. Like politicians, they should not be encouraged to believe that their behaviour changes the course of history.

3 Technique is not important. The correct approach to housekeeping may have been chiselled in granite by someone called Mother, but there is still scope for improvisation. After all, there is a correct way to kick a football, but we can't all be Norman Whiteside. Can we?

4 Clutter is worse than dirt.

5 Eggy plates, canteen medals on white shirt fronts, and cross, tearful women all respond well to a long, hot soak.

6 The smell of fresh coffee or pine disinfectant gets you Brownie points. The smell of anything burnt does not.

How To Stop Being A Housewife

Women are designed on the **Gunge-Wipe Knee-Jerk Principle**. This is the basis upon which women the world over feed anything that opens its maw, and polish anything that stands still. A man's circuits are not normally connected in this way.

Some men come as convertible models, and some don't. Some men will never change. Not if the world stops turning and Tranmere Rovers win the FA Cup. If you are married to one of these men you have bigger problems than housework. Turn immediately to the section on Tunnelling Out.

Some men will change if you make a lot of fuss. And I do mean a lot of fuss. Like pressing a Colt .45 to your temple until he wipes a few dishes. With enough persistence you can also train a flea to dance on a tightrope. Are you thinking what I'm thinking? You've got it! Why bother?

A lot of men will change if you ask them loud and clear. A lot of women think that's not a very ladylike thing to do. They sigh and sulk and drop hints instead. This is a waste of valuable time. If you want results you should lay before him a full-colour, shock-horror flow chart.

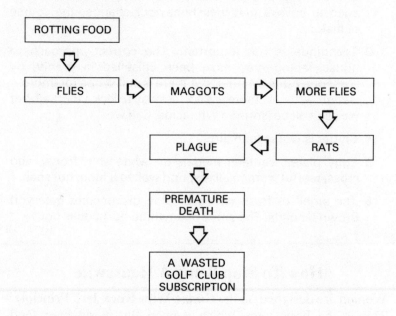

Men love to see the point.

You must tell him what needs doing and why. No need to tell him how. Any schmuck can wash a floor, and the best way for any schmuck to learn *not* to do it with a nail brush, is to do it with a nail brush.

Given the same problem, men and women come up with different solutions. Faced with a basket of ironing the size of Kanchenjunga, a thorough-going woman will think of standing at the ironing board for a very long time. A man's first thoughts are likely to be, 'What woman will do this for me out of pity? Failing that, who can I pay to do it for me? And what will it cost?' This is how people get to be President. I would never stop a man who is wandering along this track of thought. When he has worked out the logistics and the budgeting of paying for help, he will have come to a deeper understanding of washing, ironing, and matters arising.

There are other things you should know:

1 When a man questions the need for a particular job to be done at all, listen to him before you sneer. Men are sometimes smarter than women.

2 The most successful changes are made slowly. Treat any breakthrough as agreeable but unremarkable and never, under any circumstances, reward some piffling contribution like five minutes' vacuuming, with extra sex or chocolate chip icecream.

3 Ask a man to peg washing and you have the world on your back. Men will impugn his masculinity over pints of brown ale. Women you thought were your friends will offer him sanctuary and hot dinners. And his mother will tell him his bed is kept aired. Ignore them all. If you truly believe you are married to a human being who is your equal, you must support him through these difficult times. How about a peg-bag in camouflage khaki?

4 There *are* people who still scrub the front step and black-lead the grate. Man has also walked on the Moon. Do you hear what I'm saying?

5 Beware **Bungler's Law of Feigned Stupidity**. This gets passed from man to man in public bars and locker rooms, and reads as follows: *Make a big enough cock-up of any job and she will never ask you to do it again.*

6 Life is very, very short.

11

Thingummy

Bed is quite often the place where you see the funny side of marriage. It is also the place where you can be offended, furious or just downright disappointed, with the lights off.

The big thing about sex used to be, 'Is it sinful?' Then it was, 'Am I getting as much of this as other people?' Now people ask themselves, 'Shall I catch anything? Why do I feel so tired all the time? And if Pacific Dunlop acquire EBA, should I sell?' And that is not to say that the other questions have gone away. We all still suffer from shame and monotony as well. I don't know where all those adventurous, uninhibited lovers get to. I never meet any of them. I've never been to Bromley either. Maybe they're all holed up there.

When married persons talk to outsiders about sex there are four recurring themes. I applied correction factors for dishonesty, embarrassment and the effects of three double gins, but the pattern was still there:

1 Women go off the boil faster than men.

2 Some women stay off the boil for ever.

3 Women understand that men are lewd, flatulent victims of their own anatomy, but who has time for that when the oven needs cleaning?

4 Men don't understand anything.

Sex is supposed to be nice, it's supposed to be fun. If you're married it's also supposed to be exclusive, and if you're healthy it's supposed to be regular. Ideally no one should have to do anything they don't really enjoy. But, get this, you aren't meant to balk your partner's needs if you can possibly help it. You may recognise this from your childhood. It is the sexual variation of Grandma Schimmel's Rule of Nutrition by Attrition:

'I don't like knaidlach.'

'You're hungry. Eat!'

'I'm hungry but I don't like knaidlach. I'll have a Bounty Bar.'

'She doesn't like knaidlach! My mother made the best knaidlach in the stetl. I make the best knaidlach in Wood Green. It would have made me happy, but what would she know about that . . .'

'I'm sorry.'

'Never mind. You have your reasons. I shan't be here to trouble you with my cooking for many more years. It would have been nice for us to share a bowl of knaidlach, but . . .'

'I said, I'm sorry.'

'I have an idea! Just put one in your mouth! Roll it around a little. No need to swallow. Now tell me that doesn't feel good!'

When you are first married you have to try and play yourselves in. It can be interesting. Then, quite soon, you have to make it more interesting. A popular sex handbook suggests that some props might help: a six-foot clothes line, birch twigs, ceiling mirrors, a can of whipped cream, a glow-in-the-dark dildo, or the Darts Team from the Dog and Magpie? Of course, if you do this, you must remember to make sure they're all tidied away before you let Auntie Vi into your bedroom to collect her coat and hat.

68

This same guide, which incidentally I have always found to be the perfect thing for the wobbly leg on the dressing table, stresses the importance of buying the right bed. The most favourable height for a bed is so that the top of the mattress is level with the man's pubic bone. As if shopping for furniture isn't tough enough.

'Put your pubic bone against the mattress Brian.'

'I haven't got it with me.'

'*Brian*, you knew we were going to choose a bed this afternoon!'

'I thought you said you'd bring yours . . .'

A straightforward afternoon in Furniture & Electrical could turn into quite a session. You could end up in the papers.

Okay. We have the bed. Also the pillows, the contraceptives, the hardware. The dimmer switch is to hand. Now turn and take a look at what came out of the bran tub.

On this occasion, if no other, ladies first.

Girls, here is everything Claire Rayner never told you:

First, the basic-male sexual response is modelled on the Fruit Machine. You put in a dime and something happens. Sometimes you feed it all night and all you get is flashing lights. Sometimes you just show it a token and ten seconds later you're knee deep in coins. You can never tell. The one thing that is certain is that unless someone has pulled out the plug, *something* will occur.

Next, the trouser snake. Old Faithful, The Big Yin, the stuffed olive, the beef bayonet, prick, dick, tool, tadger. This is the tail that wags the dog.

A man's sexuality depends on performance. He *could* lie back and think of the Long Room at Lord's, but he would feel less of a man for doing it. His greatest sexual fear is that he won't be able to get it up. You can tell a man till you're blue in the face, that an erection is not a *sine qua non* of a good night in the sack, but there will always be a little bit of him that doesn't believe it.

So you put a coin in the machine, and for some reason all you get is a raspberry and two lemons. You may not mind at all. But he wanted to produce the big pay-out. For a man there is nothing worse than wanting to, and General Custer letting him down.

Here are some important facts.

1 In spite of the anytime anyplace stallion fantasy, all men are impotent sometimes.

2 There is hardly ever anything wrong with the hydraulics. Booze may take its toll, and certain drugs, but that's all.

3 The reason is usually psychological. Wrong woman, wrong place, thinking about it too much, trying too hard, worrying about why this is two nights running it's happened.

4 One of the best things to do about it is nothing.

5 All right, if you must do something, eat a choc ice and watch the snooker.

A man is centred on his penis. Whatever the situation, what men like is to be handled in a very direct way. Most men don't like to be touched the way most women like to be touched. *You* may like the tentative brush of a butterfly's wings, but *he* likes to be touched firmly. *Not the balls Rita! Not the balls!* For the balls we make an exception.

Oral sex is a pretty big deal. A lot of men want it, love it, can't get enough of it. A lot of women think, 'Aaargh! I should have married Norman Truscott. He would never have wanted this. And he knew how to put up shelves.'

What can I say? Instructions sound so solemn. And as a matter of fact I refuse to teach my grandmother to suck anything. I'll just say this. It is one of the few things a woman can do for a man that is more than merely physical. If his cock is his most treasured possession, your getting down there and saying, 'Hi! How ya bin?' can be quite an emotional encounter. But if you do it out of a sense of duty, with a bottle of mouthwash in your hand, it kind of loses its impact. You could always sit on it instead.

Okay fellers, you can come back in now.

Women care about details. Like who is doing it. Whether he's going to be snoring in five minutes. And whether he ever owned a toothbrush. They are far less obsessed with physical perfection than men. Which is why they are generally less responsive to erotic photography. And why they are able to respond to a beergut in jockey shorts. You may find this hard to believe, but most women do not keep a secret back-list of penile dimensions. So long as it is clean and friendly, that'll do nicely.

Women never used to have hang-ups. Pregnancy was the only drawback to married life, and a lot of women didn't mind that. A common response to 'There's another one on the way' was 'Well, a big family can be nice. And at least he won't be bothering you for a few months!'

Then someone discovered the female orgasm. Are you old enough to remember that? I think it was June 15th 1965. Its discovery created a devastating new worry – some women weren't getting any. Sex therapy was suddenly a growth industry. And so was faking it.

A woman's most important erogenous zone is her whole body. She likes open-handed men. You should avoid the furtive grab, the lunge, and the peck. And don't give the impression you have a train to catch.

Some more important facts.

1 You do not require a Davy lamp, surgical retractors, or an Ordnance Survey map to find a clitoris.

2 As questions go, 'Well did you or didn't you?' is quite a turn-off.

3 Women worry about doing it, not doing it, doing it with their mouths, other people doing it with their mouths, waking the neighbours, frightening the budgie, cellulite, thread veins, drooping breasts, and whether they turned the cooker off.

4 But, when willing, they *can* do it with the lights on, they can do it on a Wednesday afternoon, and, most surprising of all, when there's a sink full of dirty dishes.

Now for the question everyone wants to ask. **How often is everyone else doing it?** How should I know? Can you really trust anyone to tell you? A long time ago I had a friend who bought condoms once a year and never ran out. When she told me they did it once a month I thought she was being honest. Under-sexed, but honest. But, if you ask most couples, the husband says he's not getting any, and the wife says they never stop. All I can tell you is this. Men are usually at their most sexually active before the age of thirty. So, you're both mid-twenties, you get married, and three nights a week she's reading Jackie Collins and he's prodding her in the back with a broomhandle. Women peak later, sometimes not until their early forties. This is when he's reading *Custom Car* seven nights a week and she's pigging out on cheesecake.

Some people are born randy. Some go off sex at the slightest excuse. If they're worried about something or if they're angry about something, they just tune out. Women often get distracted by other things going on in their lives. Childbirth is a very good example of this. Also, major redecoration program-mes, and new titles by Jackie Collins. You don't believe me?

Girls, put up your hand if you would rather look at wallpaper samples than sleep on the wet patch. See?

Oh yes. Something else. Whatever happened to necking?

Six Things Not To Say In Bed

- Are you *sure* you have one?
- Sorry, where were we?
- Eric, can I call you back in five minutes? Something just cropped up with Thelma.
- We have another crack in the ceiling.
- Do you think it's a boil? Or could it be a carbuncle? Take a closer look.
- I *know* I'm driving you mad with lust, but do you think we should have the walls rag-rolled in Sea Haze, with an aquamarine cornice and a white festoon blind or . . .

12

Sickness and Health

Men get sick at the drop of a hat. And no matter how callous and stern you intend to be, marriage will not make any difference to their intentions. They are the principal consumers of cold cures, sticking plasters, antacids, laxatives, vitamins, extra-strength tissues, pain killers and bed rest. Men like remedies. They like them dispensed with sympathy and sensitivity. And they like them dispensed NOW.

The sickness and health marriage vow is the toughest one of all for a woman to keep. The roots of this probably run back to Mother. So many of them do. But she shouldn't take all the flak. Thirty years is plenty of time for a person to recover from chickenpox and grow up.

There is an exception to the **Standard Model Sniffler**. This is **Mr Indispensable**, who must be at his desk come hell or high water, to pass on his influenza, impetigo and broken arm to everyone he meets, and eventually succumb to heart disease with his dictaphone still in his hand.

Preventative medicine bores men. They still lag way behind women over concepts like healthy eating and dental checks when they *don't* have a toothache. You may cherish him so much you are willing to take care of these details yourself. But, don't forget, if you plan to have children, you'll be doing it for them too. Personally, I would like to take a shredder to the *Flora* advert.

There are certain ailments that are very common in the married man. Here are a few you should know about:

Garden fork through the foot. He will dine out on this for

the rest of his life and you will be forced to complete the autumn crocus planting alone.

Nasty cuts from corned beef tins. What do you expect if you stay out half the night at Conversational French and leave him to get his own tea? Corned beef tins are not to be trusted.

Strained muscles. These can come from all directions. Playing squash with someone younger, fitter and about to be promoted, showing off with a frisbee, showing off with a frisbee *and* trying to disguise a beer gut both at the same time. *Even* from attending natural childbirth classes.

And of course, there is imminent death from the common cold.

Wives get sick a lot less than husbands. Mainly they don't have the time. Wives usually hang on until they've got something really big, or they develop a chronic niggle that will be

Five Essential Items for the Care of a Sick Husband

- A house without stairs
- Ice cubes, Hot chocolate, Chicken soup like his mother used to make
- His mother, plus one large chicken
- Dr Stretchitt's Patent Ruckled Sheet Straightener
- A bottle of hard liquor

good for years and years of **silent suffering**. They are the principal users of corn plasters, elastic stockings, stimulants, tranquillisers, new lipsticks, and girl talk, so they are generally pretty cheap to run. They only break down *in extremis*, and even when the writing is truly on the wall they will not submit to the surgeon's knife until they have changed the sheets and filled the deep freeze with nourishing casseroles. Isn't this ridiculous? Even after major surgery a woman will try not to make any mess or be too much of a bother.

Women are better informed about good health than their husbands, but they often don't practice what they preach. They scream at other people to eat their greens and then have a cup of tea and a bar of chocolate for their own lunch. This is because they are too busy hemming curtains or being Secretary-General of the United Nations. And anyway, they think they're going to live for ever. Actually, they *know* they *have* to live for ever because no one else makes meat balls like they do.

There are things that wives don't like to bother their husbands with. Things arising below the belt but above the knee, if you get my drift. Funny, because men can go wrong there too, and when they do, *everyone* hears about it. Indeed it's my belief that if men started menstruating, a national emergency would be declared. But women prefer to suffer quietly. Unless it's childbirth. If we are talking childbirth, prepare to see your wife in a new light.

Of course, childbirth is not an illness. Okay, you get heartburn, morning sickness, night cramps, swollen ankles, varicose veins and a radical change of shape, metabolism and emotional outlook, but it's not an illness. She may blossom, glow and generally take to it like a brood mare, but she may not. In either event you should know this. If you attend ante-natal classes you will learn about bits of your wife you'd never dreamed of, and if you attend thoroughly modern ante-natal classes you will be invited to handle foam rubber replicas of those bits. Chin up!

Apart from dodgy, complicated and mysterious plumbing, there are two important wifely ailments you may come across. The first is brain death caused by housework. Reversible if caught early enough, but once reversed can lead to further complications such as un-made beds, and notes that say, BACK LATE. YOUR DINNER'S IN THE SUPERMARKET. The second thing is neck pain. Can be due to draughty windows, lousy theatre seats, or anxiety about tension in the Gulf, but is more usually brought on by nursing a sick husband.

Essential Items for the Nursing Husband

- A restraining harness
- A steak & kidney scented aerosol spray
- A sworn affidavit that you will not resort to the services of another woman, for *anything*
- A hiding place for all the jerseys you hot washed and all the great dishes of the world you screwed up on
- A bottle of hard liquor

── 13 ──

Fairly Happy Events

Having children is the reason I've been given more than any other for people getting married. I have seen happy, committed relationships go to the wall because one partner has made a declaration that they don't wish to have a child, ever. And I've seen marriages started, disastrously in the long run, without any discussion of whether there may or may not be children in the future. For a lot of people children are, fertility permitting, a foregone conclusion of marriage. But they shouldn't be. Because children change everything, and not always for the better. Society and Mothercare stores have romanticised the experience of starting a family. Which is not to say that having children isn't exciting and satisfying and mind-bogglingly wonderful. It is. It's also tough.

There are things you can do when you're childless that get harder when you become parents. They are connected with time, space and energy, and I'm afraid they are also connected with money. It's obvious that all-night parties will be a thing of the past. But it's not so obvious that you won't be able to soak in the bath all evening. Or that the money you used to spend on cinema tickets and popcorn will disappear on rusks and Lego starter sets. That your open-plan, split-level, dream home will be a minefield of potential injuries, and that all you'll want in the world will be eight hours' sleep, when the only thing any of us can say with any certainty, is that eight hours' sleep is what you won't get.

Couples who choose to remain childless are often accused of selfishness. I don't see that they need to defend themselves, but they do. They say that compared with people who have children they don't really want and can't really be bothered with, they rank low in the league tables of selfishness, and that the decision not to have a family does not automatically signify a psychological deviancy or the abject worship of Mammon, and I say, 'Hear! Hear!' But then, I'm not an embittered father of five whose childless brother is swanning off to Singapore for a fortnight, and I'm not a grandmother-in-waiting. Yet.

One very silly reason for having children is that your friends are all doing it. An even sillier reason is that you are closely related to someone who'd make a good granny. Women with grandmotherly ambitions are especially gifted at reminding the childless that time and ovaries wait for no one. As if we aren't all deafened by the ticking of that particular clock.

If you think you might like to have children, but you're not sure, you can have some interesting dummy runs with other people's. Just a few hours for a start, with the parents on hand to grab the steering wheel if necessary. No need to make a big thing of it. Invite round any friends with a young family, and let the afternoon unfold:

> The first thing you'll notice is that your house fills with equipment. A family consisting of two parents and a six-month old baby may take a couple of hours to unpack their car. Travel cot, high chair, baby-bouncer, baby-walker, baby-intercom, Activity Centre, nappy-changing basket, food, spare clothes, push chair . . .
>
> It's fascinating the first time you see it.
>
> The second thing you'll notice is that you can't plan to do very much.
>
> 'Fancy a walk?'
>
> 'Can't really. Rupert's due for a feed.'
>
> 'Okay. I'll play you our new Bryan Ferry album instead.'
>
> 'As long as you turn the sound down. We like Rupert to wake naturally.'

80

'Coffee?'

'Only if it's de-caffeinated. Sarah's being very careful because of her milk. And er . . . we don't want Rupert to be a passive smoker.'

'Sorry?'

'Your cigarette. Could you smoke it outside?'

'Sure. Anything else?'

'You don't happen to have a Big Bird mobile? I forgot to pack ours and Rupert's much better about having his nappy changed if he can watch Big Bird. Here we go. See how he just put his middle finger in his mouth? That means he'll wake in five minutes.'

Of course, these people have become obsessed with the minutiae of childcare in a way you never would. You're going to strap your firstborn into a papoose and get out and about. Down to the pub – Sorry, no children. Never mind, hire a boat, go out for an afternoon on the river – But what if you capsize? He might catch typhus. Or a duck might eat him! That's the trouble with this country. This country is a nation of child-haters. Nothing is geared to small children.

Why not go abroad. Foreigners love children. Book two weeks on Skorpios, get away and relax with the little lad. Just be careful of the sun, the food, the wine, and the dodgy ferry connections, and by the way, what *do* you do with a child that grizzles all the way to Gatwick?

Like I said, children change everything.

While you are deciding whether to have children, *not* having them is important.

Contraception is a very up-front subject nowadays. There are lots of methods, piles of information, and a great deal of theoretical agreement that the burden of birth control is one that should be shared. All of which does nothing to change the fact that women hate taking The Pill, and men hate using condoms. And there's something else. Women complain that men don't offer to do their bit, that a typical husband will hardly give a thought to contraception unless threatened with withdrawal of conjugals, but when a man does get out of his armchair and agree to shoulder the responsibility for a while, his wife doesn't really trust him to do it, and do it properly.

'Eric, you're not dressed for the occasion.'

'I'm just going to.'

'*Now* Eric! Put it on *now!*'

'I'm doing it.'

'Let me see. Not just out of the packet! Eric, on your finger this will prevent nothing. Now put it on!'

'I've done it.'

'That's better. Okay, you park the car and I'll go in and switch on the electric blanket.'

As soon as you decide you will have children, the emphasis changes. Instead of watching anxiously in case a period doesn't come, a girl starts watching anxiously in case it does. It's generally known that female physiology is a whimsical thing. Ovaries hate being watched and they hate to be nagged, but as soon as you take them for granted they teach you a lesson.

Aware of all this, women still panic when they don't get pregnant the first night. Two months without hitting the bull's-eye and we are talking major gynaecological crises. Three months and she starts wondering about her husband. A combination of fear, disappointment and sex out of desperation is probably the finest contraceptive ever not invented. Babies start when you least expect them to. And a year, say, liberated from pills and rubber-wear, spent trying to persuade one to start *ought* to be fun. I'm told it isn't.

Men tell me they prefer spontaneous sex to sex by thermometer. Also, when things aren't going to plan, they tend to assume that they are deficient in some way. A woman's reproductive cycle is so complex it's somehow more manageable to think, 'It must be me. Not enough lead in my pencil.' When you are losing sleep having thoughts like that, it doesn't help to be woken at five and asked to do a curtain call. 'Eric! Wake up! If you get a move on now we can fit it in twice before work!'

A great many women know when they are five minutes' pregnant. Men find this incredible and unnerving, but that's how men feel about a lot of womanly talents. Other women are also very good at sensing the presence of a new life:

'Jill's pregnant, then.'
'When did she tell you that?'
'She didn't.'
'When did Keith tell you?'
'He didn't.'
'Have you been sneaking a look at their mail?'
'No need. You can tell by the serene way she mopped up that soup.'

'Are you crazy! Is this some new pregnancy test I missed?'

'Not just that! She was surrounded by an aura of burgeoning spirit, and she didn't touch her coffee. How come men are so stupid?'

According to Hollywood legend, the first hint you get that a woman has a little secret, is she faints. This bit of nonsense evolved because cinematographically, fainting looks better than throwing up. Fainting is usually due to wearing your belt too tight, having black coffee and a cigarette for breakfast, and air-conditioning being non-existent on the Northern Line. The commonest symptom of **pregnancy** is a missed period, which at least has the advantage that strangers don't try to force your head between your knees.

After a missed period comes nausea, low libido, and a longing to fall asleep on your feet.

Thinking you may be pregnant but not knowing for sure, is a curious limbo for both parties. You find yourself observing small children on trains with a new interest, and then stopping yourself, in case it's bad luck.

As soon as a pregnancy is confirmed, a woman is drawn into a complicated rite of passage. Certain aspects of her life will be mapped out for her by professionals and experts. Other women will talk to her in a new language. And she will end up with a good idea what is expected of her. For some expectant fathers this is not so. A great drama is being played out, and he watches most of it from the wings. If he's lucky he may be entrusted with a very small walk-on part, like being asked to assemble a cot, but mainly he will be asked to be silent and brave while matters of life and death are decided, centre-stage.

But a man can be as involved as he wants to be. The traditional role – increasing his life assurance cover and then maintaining a physical and emotional distance from what is going on inside his wife's enormous dungarees – is still the one chosen by a surprising number of men. I say surprising, because this is no longer the jammy option. There are pressures from all quarters for a man to get right in there and live the pregnancy as though it were his own.

Some men want to do it anyway. They take to it naturally. A lot of men roll up their sleeves, do their homework, and try to get straight As, because that's the easiest way to ensure a quiet life. Hand on their heart, they would really prefer to go to the pub or play football.

For seven years I taught ante-natal classes. First to women, and then, increasingly, to women and men together. Most of the men who came to my classes would have summed up their reasons like this: 'My wife is pregnant. I love my wife. If she thinks this is a good idea, I'll go along with it. Any chance of us finishing before closing time?'

The main reason I stopped teaching those classes was that I noticed something. My teaching time was getting shorter, and the coffee breaks were getting longer. Word got round, and I had waiting lists of people who wanted to enrol with me because they'd heard I gave such terrific coffee breaks. Came one evening, I was all prepared to do my Oscar-winning demonstration of the second stage of labour and they refused to re-convene. The women were talking sore nipples, and the men were engrossed in knee injuries, so I just topped up the percolator. No one even noticed me retire.

The things men and women need to know about each other in pregnancy and childbirth, can be summarised on the back of a box of Nappikleen.

Pregnant women get happy, excited, frightened, sick, tired, swollen, droopy, randy, frigid, constipated, and amazingly perky. Sometimes all in one morning.

Physically, pregnancy is not merely a case of a bigger bosom and a much bigger belly. The whole body is affected. Even the finger nails. Emotionally she changes as well. She would like to feel mature, competent, desirable and safe, but mainly she will just settle for safe.

Pregnant men also get happy, excited, randy and constipated. They don't get frightened. They get terrified. Also, neglected, jealous, guilty, baffled, useless, and euphoric. All this *and* there's a nursery needs wallpapering.

Instead of stilted talks and guided tours round labour wards, I would like to see hospitals offering expectant fathers Mass Thumb-Sucking Sessions. They could all huddle together for comfort on the relaxation mats while the girls went off into another room to compare stretch marks.

Not being present at the birth of your child is considered bad form these days. This is a pity. One of the advantages of being a father should be the freedom to choose:

'Yes, I had *planned* on being there. Been to all the classes, practised the breathing and so forth, but then the night Ruth started they were repeating that marvellous Dennis Potter thing, you know, the one with the detective and that skin complaint, and the thing was we do intend to have other children at some future date, whereas you never know about a Dennis Potter, especially with the BBC . . .'

And the same courtesy, the same freedom of choice, should be extended to women. Some of them prefer to do it on their own:

'Ruth, you're doing brilliantly! I'll just give your back a bit of a rub and then I'll read you some more Margaret Drabble. Breathe, darling, breathe! Relax those shoulders! Remember what your teacher said about the perineum stretching like the gently unfolding petals of a flower!'

'Dominic . . .'

'Darling?'

'Piss off.'

Officially, childbirth is divided into three stages. Five would be more accurate:

1 Early First Stage

This begins at about two in the morning, after a very heavy week at work, and solitary consumption of a bottle of Australian red. During this stage the labouring woman gets up, re-packs her suitcase, hoovers, defrosts the fridge and launders all the curtains. Meanwhile, man sleeps. This is all for the best. The only useful function for a man at this time is to ensure that he has a car, taxed, roadworthy and ready to go without hand-cranking.

2 Middle First Stage

This is when it starts to hurt. It is the latest point at which a woman will want to play chess, or choose names. If she is under the influence of analgesics she will divide her time equally between dozing and blaspheming. But this will change. For the worse. Gradually she will doze less and curse more, as she moves into Late First Stage.

3 Late First Stage *Also known as 'Never Again, You Animal!'*

This phase of labour should carry an X Certificate. It hurts, anywhere on the scale between agonising and unendurable. This is not the time to remind a labouring woman about spiritual growth through suffering. It isn't the time to do anything. Don't touch her. Don't even look at her. Conceal yourself behind a pile of sterile drapes and listen to the language. This is the girl you married. Daddy's Little Princess.

4 Second Stage

The second stage of labour is amazing. A baby's head is the size of a Jaffa grapefruit. And you know which way it's coming out? No zippers. No Velcro. And they say men are brave!

5 Third Stage

This stage of labour begins when the mother is safely delivered of two pounds of lamb's liver and an old cellophane wrapper. What happens next, roughly in sequence, is you make a series of emotional phone calls, you buy a bunch of flowers, you go home, try to mollify the cat, and feel very lonely. Then you start sweating. About road safety, teddy bears with loose eyes, and nuclear annihilation. This stage lasts approximately the rest of your life.

14

Can We Talk?

Women have the reputation of being incapable of silence. This is a vile slander. The hills are alive with the sound of male voices. Listen.

The only place women really talk is in the company of other women. In mixed company women invariably back off and leave it to the men. Some men apply the worst kinds of thuggery in order to grab the spotlight and keep it, but there's really no need. Most women are more than ready to hand it to them on a nice clean plate.

Here we have yet another vitally important difference between women and men. Men communicate for practical reasons. To draw attention to themselves, to elucidate certain facts, or to convey an urgent message, such as, 'Park in that space, drongo, and you're a dead man!' Women do a lot of their communicating with the sole purpose of making other people feel good. They are great users of 'Hm . . . hm . . . uhuh . . . yeah? . . . And then?' *All* of these are perfectly valid uses for the human voice. The trouble is, when a man and a woman speak to each other they find they are separated by the myth of common language.

When a wife asks her husband about world trends in superconductor sales, she is very likely doing it because she just told him why Mr Bighorn came back early from Corfu, and now she feels it's only fair he should tell her something. Women think that conversations should be like long rallies in lawn tennis, with the words dropping nicely, first one side of the net, then the other. But if a man sees the chance of three game points, even against his wife, he'll take them. He'll interrupt, because he hates a slow build-up. He'll tell her about the sales figures and move on without pause to why he'll never buy Fuel Injection again, world peace, and why the only time he could get a squash court was three in the morning.

There is another important difference. Men generally express themselves clearly. Women can learn a lot from this. They find it hard to criticise or refuse or dismiss, except in a very indirect manner.

'Would you like time to shower before dinner?' she says. What she really means is 'Get out of that shirt you've been wearing all week, otherwise I refuse to eat in the same room.' But she has tried to say it nicely, because oiling wheels was one of the first womanly skills she learned at her mother's knee.

'No,' he says. 'I don't want to shower before dinner.'

The result? Her point got lost in the niceties. His didn't. He didn't want to shower, and he said as much. The stinking scumbag.

It isn't very surprising that many men believe when a woman says, 'No,' she means, 'Yes,' or at least, 'Maybe.' The coy, pouting body language women use without realising it gets very confusing. The finest example of this is an angry woman. Most women, at some stage in the making of an angry statement, will smile. Her smile is shorthand for 'The message may be strong meat, but it is being delivered by a sweet compliant little lady. Can I make you a cup of tea as soon as we've finished the nasty business?' Then they wonder why they don't get taken seriously.

Women say, 'No,' and they *do* mean it, but deep inside they can hear Mother saying, 'How callous! How unpleasant! Nice girls don't do this!' And it shows. They *can* overcome it but it takes a lot of effort. Probably the emotional equivalent of learning to bump ski. When a man talks to a woman he would do well to bear this in mind. Think of it as a mild disability, which some women are better at overcoming than others. After all, men have a handicap too. Men are poor listeners.

The better you listen, the more sensitive you are to the mood of what's being said, and to what is *not* being said. Women are well-practised in this field. Listening in to the same conversation a typical woman will glean a hundred times more from it than a typical man. Men find this incredible. They call it Feminine Intuition, but any man can learn it. It's a simple matter of engaging the brain and ear, and restraining the tongue. Probably no harder than a manual gear change.

So men and women use talk differently. For a man, talk is a simple, unemotional way of keeping a grip on the air waves until he thinks of something startling to share with the world.

You can see the sense of it. It's like not shutting down a blast furnace unless it's staying shut for ever, because it'll take you a fortnight to get it going again. They talk and talk, to stay in shot, and any subject will do so long as it isn't How It Feels To Be A Bloke. That one is taboo. Sorry, but there we are. Men want their feelings to be understood without having to talk about them. The British fish-waste industry didn't get where it is today by its visionaries sitting around engaged in fluent emotional exchange.

Women like to talk about emotions and anxieties. They see the occasional bit of self-disclosure as a good thing. I agree with them. But then, I am a woman. The problem with talk of this kind is that you can only ever indulge in it with other women. There *are* men, I've read about them in *Woman's Own*, who'll open up but they are so few they're all booked up for years ahead. Getting an audience with one of them is one degree harder than getting tickets for *Cats*.

There are some people you should know about, otherwise you might marry one of them:

First, the woman whose voice is on a loop recording. Not to be mistaken for the normal woman who breaks silence once every seven years and reduces everyone to such a state of shock that she *appears* to be monopolising the spoken word world-wide.

Loop-recording Women are abnormal. They move randomly through subjects. What they say is unpunctuated, and it is said oblivious to response, and fast. Sometimes too fast for the human ear: Cat food, Zionism, uterine prolapse, Gordon the Gofer, Dundee cake, Rastafarianism, chilblains, Esther Rantzen, recent advances in genetic engineering, cat food, Zionism . . .

There is some kind of pathology at the root of this. A worn flange on the speech regulator, or a cracked circuit board. It will slow down with old age, but there's not much you can do with a woman like this if she's in her prime. You must get away sometimes. If you don't, you'll become violent. Take separate holidays. Hide in a sound-proofed potting shed. And don't worry about offending her. She has been inoculated against rudeness and rejection. If the ballroom at Blenheim Palace emptied because of her, she would still bang on . . . dandruff, Kurt Waldheim, nylon pan-scrubs, Lamarckian Evolutionary Theory, dandruff . . .

She couldn't stop if she tried.

Not like the **Barrack Room Lawyer**.

I believe **Barrack Room Lawyers** are always men. I've never met a female one, and I've been around.

Some of them do marry. Heaven knows how. A forty-year sentence to be served in an echo-chamber would do a lot more good. It would be a pleasure for them, and a relief for others. The principal feature of a BRL is that he holds the only correct opinion on every subject known to man. You can even invent something, a hypothetical task to perform, or problem to solve, and he will have it taped. He differs from all those men who keep talking because they're certain they're about to find something important to say. *He* has already found it.

He likes to begin sentences with, 'If you'll be guided by me,' and, 'Luckily for you I can be of some help on this one.' He also uses, 'Correct me if I'm wrong.' But be warned. He doesn't mean that.

The good thing about these men is that they often do know something useful. Especially about Consumer Rights, obscure local government statutes, and the working parts of aeroplanes . . .

'You see *there*, that's where the air gets drawn in . . .'

'I hope we don't have a big hold-up in Immigration.'

'Then, the fuel expands in the combustion chamber, and the turbine utilises some of that energy to drive the compressor . . .'

93

'Connie was two hours in Immigration last time she went.'

'But most of that gaseous energy goes to develop the propulsive thrust. If you'll be guided by me, you'll let me have that window seat. Now the turbo-prop engine is different. Not a lot of people know that, so I'll explain it to you. You've got two concentric shafts . . .'

If you have married one of these men, never fly. Never get involved in litigation, protocol, or games of Scrabble. And never, under any circumstances whatsoever, enter into a discussion as to the best route from Kenilworth to Grimsby. If you'll be guided by me, that is.

Finally, **Silent Man**, **Taciturn Man**. Don't be fooled. Out there where it counts, he can give as good as he gets. You may be married to someone who comes home, lights his pipe and never says more than, 'Hrmph,' but you should see him in the Works Canteen. Barging into the middle of sentences, fouling to gain possession of the subject, then booting it away because he's thought of another one he finds more interesting. Man to man he is a beast.

'I'd say a man who is silent at home is best left that way. Keep him up to date with brief, pithy bulletins. *We're expecting a baby mid-July. I'm not cooking tonight. The roof just blew off.* For conversation, make friends with a woman.

He-Speak / She-Speak

When a man says:

- I don't want to watch *Kramer versus Kramer* again.
- This pie is wonderful, but I'm not hungry.
- Your sister gets up my nose.

he means it.

When a woman says:

- Tell me how you feel.
- Crying is very therapeutic.
- Gimme a hug.

so does she.

When she says:

My back aches, how much extra time are they playing in this match, and I wonder what a bottle of Ma Griffe costs these days? she is actually saying: 'Why don't you switch off the TV, empty the dustbin, and acknowledge my existence you jerk!'

When a man says:

'That bastard Hislop is going to get the Lufthansa account, my tongue hurts, his doughnut is bigger than mine, for the love of Christ just fix me some milk of magnesia!' he really means: 'Aaaargh! Don't let the big boys get me!'

15

...And Another Thing

Right from the start we should distinguish – *Are you listening to me?* – we should distinguish between arguments and rows. If you have a lot of them you have probably forgotten the difference, but there is one.

An argument is a type of discussion. It is often an on-going feature of marriage. It arises because you hold differing opinions on something – politics, ethics, the best way to crack nuts – and neither of you feels able to surrender any ground. I have been arguing with my poor benighted husband for sixteen years, about whether there is anything to be said in praise of Geoffrey Boycott. We both know we shall never make any progress in this dispute, but it does give us something to do when rain stops play.

I know a couple who have been arguing for twenty-seven years about which of them has the most slovenly domestic habits. As with most long-running arguments between husband and wife, there is a strong element of humour underpinning their righteous indignation. Arguments of this kind can be very entertaining when conducted in public. In fact there is nothing to choose between this couple. They are both highly accomplished slovens. They say, 'Stay for supper,' and then squabble for hours because the cupboard is bare. No one else is the least surprised. At a convenient moment one of us slips out to the Take Away, another washes some plates and moves the piles of old newspapers from chairs. The two protagonists are oblivious. It's as though they're slogging it out for the very first time, and each is willing to defend his reputation to the death.

I'm pretty well in favour of arguments. There are people who like to pretend marriage is a haven of peace and tranquillity. Personally I like to see signs of life. Twenty-five years and never a cross word? Can you believe that? I don't know much about Probability Theory, well actually I don't know *anything* about Probability Theory, but what would you think are the chances of living together through all the stormy seas of life and never getting the urge to re-educate your partner on the superiority of men, women, foreign cars, or *your* method of filling in a pools coupon? I'd say slim. I'd say what we have here is a true marriage of Doormat and Tyrant. Someone who never expresses a contrary opinion on anything, is married to someone who is so enchanted by the sound of their own voice they don't notice the lack of animated response. I'm not really knocking it. I think it's a shame and a bore, and I'm certain there must be a high incidence of gastric ulcers amongst the doormat population, but so many people prefer it that way, who am I to say they shouldn't?

Rows are something else. A row is a flare-up. A storm in a teacup. Important subjects may first be brought up in the course of a row, but they can only be dealt with thoroughly by long arguments. Years long. It is an important distinction. The fact that your partner knows only two lines from *Rigoletto* and, since it's up for discussion, he doesn't even know those *accurately*, is good basic row material. Given time and a wider canvas it has the makings of a good argument. Something like this could last you well into retirement, bickering over Verdi from your bath-chairs. But, more than likely, you won't bother because it was just a row, a one-off. Next time you'll be rowing because one of you finished the last of the orange juice and didn't say. *Rigoletto* will be ancient history.

Some people have a physical need to row. If they go without a barney for more than a few days they get tense. They could take the dog for a walk, but they don't. They pick on someone. Usually their nearest and dearest.

It is possible to prevent a row. You just walk out on it. This is
bellum interruptum. Only try it if your timing is very good
indeed, and make sure you take with you your coat, your keys,
and enough money for a cup of coffee or a night at the Hilton,
Park Lane. It's a mean, frustrating stroke to pull. You cannot
have a row on your own. Trust me, I tried it. But if you are
feeling delicate you should not be obliged to weather a Force
Niner, all because the white of his egg wasn't properly cooked.
Go out. Stay out.

Putting your hands over your ears won't help. You may not
be able to hear what's being said, but you can still feel what's
being thrown.

I had a girlfriend who used to defuse explosive domestic scenes by taking off her clothes. If it was one of those days, if someone had filled in his crossword, or he could only find itchy socks to wear, off it all came. The time he got constipated and his stock fell twenty-four points, she was hardly dressed all week. I have to tell you this has never worked for me. If you too have a body that looks like you're wearing a life-belt and jodhpurs when you're not, do as I do. Use the Exit Left, carrying cheque book and car keys, Technique.

A public row can be very nasty, not least for the onlookers. I find them embarrassing. Even the time when a steak knife was brandished, what I chiefly felt was embarrassment. We were only there for a glass of sherry. And it wasn't a good old knock-about argument about sticking a SDP poster in the bay window. It was a row. About affording a holiday. Maybe I'm old-fashioned, but I don't think steak knives are quite polite at sherry parties.

This is often half the trouble. Unnatural social situations are a breeding ground for fights. Beautiful people are especially prey to them. They are under so much pressure to look and act beautiful on all occasions that they crack.

A long time ago we knew some beautiful people. She used to have manicures, and in those days only visiting Americans in lime green pant-suits went in for manicures. She also had dinner parties. Walnut table, candle-lit, the HP Sauce decanted into a lead crystal bowl, and a choice of *three* puddings. The burden of stage-managing these grand affairs, of inviting the right people, taking risks with fennel, and at all times looking radiantly married, was too much. Of course it was. There was always an air of suppressed menace when they opened the door. They would keep disappearing into the kitchen. Drawers would be slammed, words spat under cover of the Herb Alpert records, and every dinner ended the same way. An angry flush on her throat, a homicidal glitter in his eye. Signs of unfinished business.

If you are allergic to public rows, I'd strongly recommend you give up dinner parties. I did, and I never felt better.

Christmas is another tinder-box. Expense, claustrophobia, gift-wrapped evidence of other people's loathsome taste, too much food, too much Agatha Christie, too many reminders about peace, goodwill and joy to all mankind. It is probably inescapable. Even if you posted your cards and then caught a plane to Acapulco, Christmas would catch up with you. Lying poolside you'd suddenly think, 'December 25th already! Time for a row about ice cubes. Time to admit I forgot to buy batteries, cherry brandy, and a four-hour videotape.

After years of meticulous research I can reveal that the **five main sources of Christmas strife** are:

1 Turkey – size of

2 Turkey – foolproof cooking methods of

3 Turkey – tastiest parts, fair division of

4 Turkey – trendy, high-fibre attempts to dispense with

5 Relations – abominable, other people's.

But there is something else. Christmas is perfectly possible without turkey and uncles. The inescapable part of it is the interruption of normal life. No buses to run for, no perpetually ringing telephone to curse. We get withdrawal symptoms. We get the sweats, the shakes. We start a row. If you have ever spent Boxing Day planning your divorce, try this. Go out on a limb. Do something non-festive. Queue to use your Cashpoint card. Watch a really grisly Panorama, a Budget Day Special maybe, that you have taped and saved for the occasion. Or clean a Venetian blind. The possibilities are endless. And just a couple of hours away from the advocaat and 'The Two Ronnies' can save you weeks in Marriage Guidance.

100

The most vulnerable witnesses to marital rows are children, animals of a nervous disposition and friends. Especially single friends, for whom any aspect of marriage presents a baffling conundrum. Friends can come off very badly in a row. They can be asked to take sides.

'Did you hear that? Did you hear her accuse me of not pulling my weight in the garden? I never stop! I practically never get out of my wellies! Miriam, you're a reasonable woman. Would *you* say I did my fair share out there?'

'Don't drag her into it. The fence is nearly falling down, the lawn needs edging, the pond has turned green. You stroll out, stare into the cold-frame, dib a few holes with your dibber and then slide off to watch the racing from Doncaster! Miriam, you're a reasonable woman. Is he a skiver, or what?'

This is a low trick. Married people who want to keep their friends should never stoop to this. They should say, 'Miriam, we just have to go into the next room and abuse one another. Do fix yourself a drink. We shouldn't be long.'

Men often ask me, 'Laurie, what about **Pre-menstrual tension**?' I always reply 'Pre-menstrual! Who's pre-menstrual!' and then, with an offensive weapon in my hand, 'You think I've got hormones? I'll show you who's got hormones! One more crack about the time of the month and I'm gonna spread your entire endocrine system over this wall!'

No, seriously, we should talk about it.

Women who are reproductively active have a cyclic physiology, sometimes reflected by their mood and temperament. It's only noticeable because it comes round every twenty-eight days. Men are cyclic too. Their cycle starts about thirty seconds after birth and is completed for the first time with the onset of *rigor mortis*. Along the way they get shitty, weep, scream, can't get their trousers to fasten, and start world wars. Because this

101

can take upward of seventy years no one has written to *The Lancet* about it, or opened a clinic with a view to curing it. It's all a question of perspective.

Unfortunately, PMT has become another designer disease. Looking for a complaint with your name on it? Dyslexia? Bulimia? Or how about three days a month wanting to rub out the world and draw it again? PMT could be the one for you. Some people suffer from it permanently. They are surrounded from sparrow fart to bat squeak by knaves, fools and unworkable systems. Arthur Scargill could have a very interesting hormonal profile.

If you are married to someone who suffers pre-menstrual tension, there are a few things that should be made clear. First, who made the diagnosis? If you did, if it is your very own privately held theory, keep it that way. Second, if in the course of a single day she loses a contract, an ear-ring, and her faith in automatic washing machines, is it helpful or relevant for you to check the calendar? And third, exactly what is *your* rating in the charm and placidity stakes?

The trouble with rows is the aftermath. If you've been got at, it's only natural to want to strike back. If it was you who started it, you have to find a way to say Sorry.

Striking back can take many forms. If you seek instant gratification, **Revenge through Psycho-analysis** may be your best bet. The nub of this method is 'You're not bad, you're mad.' Important buzz words are Inadequacy and Insecurity. Used with the correct measures of kindly wisdom and regret, a little session of this will take the wind out of anyone's sails.

'I only said I didn't like the way you had your hair cut.'
'That's all right. You can't help the way you are.'
'But the more I look at it, the more it grows on me.'
'I should be more patient. When a man is bonded so destructively with a mother who won't let go, he's not conscious of how disabled he is in relationships with real women.'
'Know something? When you're riled your hair looks terrific!'
'So how did it feel to be castrated at puberty?'

An alternative to this is **Total Recall of all Wrongs**:

'I didn't mean it the way it sounded.'
'Carry on! Be my guest! What's a little criticism of my sexual prowess, after nineteen years of jealousy, obsessiveness, scraping the near-side wing of the only Austin Healey I ever owned, and refusing to buy me *Penthouse* when I had both legs in traction!'

Or there is **silence**. But for how long? A haunted stare into the ruins of the rest of your life is brilliant for half an hour. Longer than that and you really need lessons from the French Lieutenant's Woman.

And what about **Cold Bum**? Many couples make a rule that the sun must not set on hostilities. Come bedtime they kiss and make up. That's good. I go along with that. Cold Bum causes insomnia. Lying awake wondering if she's wondering if you're wondering . . .

Far better to clear the air and get a decent night's sleep. The real surprise comes the first time you go to bed friends and *wake up* to Cold Bum. If like me you talk in your sleep, this can happen a lot:

'Pass the milk please. So who's Randolph?'

'Dunno.'

'You seemed to know who he was at three o'clock this morning. And four. And five.'

'I don't know anyone called Randolph.'

'So do you usually have such a good time with people you never heard of called Randolph?'

'Dunno.'

'Maybe it was Gandalf. Who've you been seeing called Gandalf?'

I refuse to have anything to do with rows like this. How can you defend yourself when you can't even remember seeing the movie? Of course, you can always save it for when you feel the need to strike back – a combined Revenge by Psycho-analysis *and* Naming of All Previous Convictions:

'My fault. I should make more allowances for a person whose ability to fantasise is so impoverished they have to hijack what other people say in their sleep!'

Well . . . none of us is a saint.

Conversational English
Lesson 32 – *Useful responses for husbands and wives*

'And what time do you call this? I work my fingers to the bone, never a word of thanks, your dinner's ruined, and another thing . . .'
'Signals failure, Bethnal Green.'

'Go on, go on, hit a defenceless man!'
'First come out of the wardrobe.'

'Come along then. I really want to hear the rest of this crackpot theory.'
'You're going to, don't worry!'

'That's it! I'm going out!'
'Oh, no, you're not!'

'Maybe I'll stay in tonight.'
'Okay. What's going on?'

'I'm a very sick man.'
'You are drunk.'
'I only had a couple of beers with Malcolm.'
'You are an animal.'
'I'm an animal.'
'I'll get you an Alka-Seltzer, you poor thing.'
'I *am* a poor thing. And beer makes me very randy.'
'You are a disgusting, inconsiderate, salacious slug, and I should have listened to my mother.'

16

Love Me, Love Muriel

When you first fall in love there are some nice spin-offs. You have a spring in your step. Things don't get you down the way they normally would. And you eat less. With my friend Gloria you can tell exactly what stage she's at in a romance by a quick look at her waistline. If she's wearing Evans Outsize she's between men. But when she's in love she can do a large 10. Or so she tells me. I've never seen it with my own eyes because when love is in the air you don't see Gloria. She forgets her friends.

This is a very familiar story. Friendship, and a wide and varied social life are the first casualties of romance. Suddenly you don't have time for all that any more. You are utterly absorbed with each other. And for a little while that's natural. For a very little while. Soon one of you has to put your head outside the door and see what's going on. There are things you have to get on with. If you don't pay your bills, the gas man will cut you off, and if you never call your friends so will they. Anyway, the human body can't stand many weeks of unremitting dopeyness. So you start weaning yourselves. Setting yourselves little tests to see whether a few hours apart causes heart failure. And eventually, when you return to a kind of reality, you remember that you used to have some friends. Dear dependable Muriel. Good old Stan. And what do you have to do next? What you have to do next is invite Muriel and Stan round so you can show them why you've been listed as a missing person. Introduce them to your chosen partner in life. Perform the acid test. Or as we scientists prefer to say 'Expose the new material to **a rigorous Stan-and-Muriel**.'

A lot of people skip this stage in a romance. They go to Rimini for a fortnight, meet something in a sunhat, woo it, bed it, swear their undying love, land at Gatwick and grab a cab straight into Horsham so they can knock up a sleeping jeweller and buy a ring. They are in love. They are totally compatible. They share interests in spaghetti, and sun tans, and drinks made out of Sambuca, Pepsi and liquid paraffin, and really heaps of other subjects. Obviously the thing for them to do is make a permanent commitment to one another *immediately*.

This, I have to say, is tragic. A few simple precautions can save so much heartache. It's like buying a second-hand car. Would you do that without getting Merv the Marv to crawl under it and check for rust? Of course you wouldn't. This relationship, this intended marriage, if subjected to a cheap and swift Stan-and-Muriel, will turn out to have as many surprises as a seven-year-old Escort. It's a tough thing to do when you think you've found perfection, but you'll be glad you did. Friends see through all the whistles and bells. And they know how many beans make five.

I nearly married a man once. It wasn't a whirlwind holiday romance. In fact it was a bit like a cold start with no choke, but once we got going we only had time for each other. When we weren't looking into each other's eyes our hours were spent admiring his bank book and going for long country walks. You can't avoid friends for ever. Eventually I had to do a Stan-and Muriel. Actually I just did a Muriel.

She said, 'Laurie, you are insane. This man wears Brylcreem.'

'Does he?' I said. 'I've never noticed. He's usually wearing a deerstalker.'

'And that's another thing,' said Muriel, 'What's with all these walks? You're not supposed to go to the country. You're not even supposed to go as far as Ongar. You're allergic to cows,

107

sheep, any place you can't walk in three-inch heels and *fifteen* different types of grass!'

She was so right. It had all just slipped my notice, what with love and everything.

You must **listen to your friends**. Tell them, 'This is Shirley. We're thinking of getting married.' No need to mention her cookery certificates. Friends will always go to the heart of things.

'Seems like a nice girl. I don't suppose there's anything can be done about her brain?'

If your friends think she's thick, she must be very thick, because for them she will have been trying her hardest. If your friends think you've fallen for a wimp or a shark or a secret lemonade drinker, they are very probably right. Being friends they will stick by you whatever you decide to do, but they will then have to do the other thing friends are obliged to do and say, 'I told you so!'

If you agree, sensibly, to introduce your partner to your friends at an early stage, you'll find that you'll get a much more thorough report from a Muriel than you will from a Stan. It's something women have a gift for.

A man friend will confine himself to practical questions. Is this person from the right kind of family? What will be the size of the marriage settlement? And does this mean you won't be joining him at Cheltenham for the Gold Cup?

A woman friend will look at the attractive shop window your loved one is presenting to the world and be able to spot right away what's been bundled out of sight. She'll be able to tell you if you're about to marry the kind of girl who'll slash her wrists the first time you're late home. She'll be able to tell you if you're marrying the kind of man who'll throw a tantrum if his slippers aren't warming every evening for the rest of his life. Neurotics, philanderers, bullies, whiners, nothing escapes the notice of a good woman friend. Furthermore, that same good friend will be there to remind you that each of us chooses one basic mistake in life, and then keeps on making it.

'Irene! I think we've been here before a few times! I think what we have here, Irene, is another Mother's Boy.'

'But he makes me feel so good!'

'Yes, I'm definitely experiencing *déja vu*. Okay. Just do one small thing for me, Irene. Will you check that at least he's toilet-trained? *Irene?*'

In the end we all marry someone imperfect. Even our wise friends. Then we have to live in a triangle. You, your partner and your friends.

Traditionally, men managed this aspect of marriage much better than women did. They kept up their contacts, through work and through clubs, and women just stayed home. They felt intoxicated if they exchanged two words with the butcher's boy. The first examples of married women I ever saw conformed to this pattern. My mother's generation, married during the war, worked long and hard with dusters and carpet beaters once they were no longer needed to beat Adolf Hitler. There was no time for talking to other women. My mother had friends, but they were all in the same boat as she was. I didn't really know who my mother's friends were until she was widowed and so, in time, were some of them. They had about forty years talking to catch up on.

I knew my father's friends, though. I could put faces to their names, some from the war, most from his school days. He certainly talked to other men. It may have been mainly about whether Compton should have been re-called for the Oval Test when he had a dodgy knee, or the best way to repack a gland nut, but at least they talked. The channels were open.

In most marriages things are now very different. Women have overtaken their husbands in their ability to maintain a network of friends. They've put down their dusters. Result? More dust, less isolation. For women this has been a good thing and indirectly you might have expected it to be a good thing for the men in their lives. Instead of waiting tight-lipped for the sound of the key in the latch, women now think, 'Stuff this! I'll see if Jen fancies a swift half of red.'

Here we have **the makings of marital strife**. We have come to a fundamental difference between the sexes.

It doesn't often happen that a tired woman comes home to a houseful of laughing, chattering men, but let's suppose one did. Would she confiscate the corkscrew? Would she slam every door in the house until *someone* paid her some attention? Would she go down with beri-beri, right there and then? No. She'd think, 'Great! I'll sling myself a frozen dinner in the microwave, and have a nice early night.' She'd make sure someone knew the whereabouts of a mop, a bucket and a bottle of disinfectant, and go and devote a whole evening to her own pleasure.

Without special training, only the most exceptional men can behave in this way. I'd guess it's to do with a strongly developed sense of territory. There's a big lump of the male brain dedicated to 'This is *my* house. There's *my* chair. And there's *my* spaniel and *my* wife. God, why have you been so good to me? Oh no! The spaniel has piddled on *my* rug! This is the trouble with *my* wife. She never takes *her* spaniel for a walk.' When those brain cells detect alien women encroaching on a man's territory, they go into a frenzy of electro-chemical activity. 'Come on! Gimme a break! I took a big hit today. What I need is to sit in my shorts and watch some TV till Wall Street closes. What I don't need is a Mothers' Meeting.'

Worse still if the visiting woman is single. 'Doesn't she have a date tonight? How come? Is she a dyke or what? I *mean*, is there something we should know?'

A single woman friend is like sweating gelignite. Anything could happen. And yet it hardly ever does. (You try to fix them up and how do they repay you? They call you the next day and say, 'Before you introduce me to anyone else called Abe who is handsome and witty, would you kindly check with me first what is my idea of witty, not to mention handsome?')

Divorced women friends are even worse. They cast a cynical eye over everyone else's marriage. They tell home truths, and sabotage a nicely planned table. Not that you'd dare invite them anyway. If they're prepared to unglue a marriage, who can say what they might do to a dinner party!

The whole Marriage-Friendship question reeks of subversion. Women know that men try to subvert one another. Into staying until Last Orders are called. Into going to Tibet for the next World Cup. There is nothing new under the sun.

Men know that women try to subvert one another. They're just not sure what about. I'll tell you. They goad one another into grabbing life by the balls. If you are ever greeted by, 'I'm going overland to India, and when I get back I'm doing Psychology with the Open University. Also, I got rid of my blue eye-shadow and I'm now charging £2 an hour for ironing shirts,' you can be sure of one thing. She had lunch with a friend.

We all want other people to love our friends as much as we do. Well, *almost* as much. Unless you are in with one of those crowds that swaps car keys on Saturday nights, you don't want your partner getting too enthusiastic about your best friend. Here there is a fine line to be trod:

'Nice evening.'
'Hm.'
'Fran's a great girl.'

'She certainly is!'
'What do you mean?'
'Great . . . presence, personality . . .'
'When did she show you her personality?'
'Of all your friends she's always been my favourite.'
'I'll kill her.'

See? With a Fran like that, who needs enemies?

17

Playing Away

I would argue with those who say that the marriage vow of **fidelity** is the hardest one to keep. I'd have said that the one about sharing all your worldly goods with someone who doesn't even begin to understand the value of a collection of pre-war model cars was a much tougher one. Or what about the ones in fine print about washing twenty-two muddy football strips and helping with the cricket teas in a floral pinny, that you don't even remember making? In my book those are the real stinkers.

But a lot of people do have problems with being sexually faithful. On bad days it can seem like the whole world is screwing around. Then you realise, for a lot of them it's wishful thinking.

I have to say I'm not surprised extra-marital affairs are so popular. Marriage is a long haul, and it's usually under-taken when both partners are in their twenties. When I was in my twenties I liked my husband and, amongst other things, long hair, flared trousers, poems by Leonard Cohen, and two sugars in my coffee. Now I'm in my forties I still like my husband, but he's the only survivor from that list. So, I was better at choosing people than I was at choosing hair styles? I hope so. But that's not really the point. The point is that we all change with time, and if sex is any part of our lives it isn't very surprising that our sexual tastes change as well.

We should begin with those people who never take an extra-marital lover in the whole of their lives. I have made this artistic decision more out of realism than moralism. It is impossible to know the numbers involved because you can't trust everyone to tell you the truth, but my guess is that the majority of marriages are faithful, *technically* at least. Partly this must be due to a genuine sense of commitment on both sides. A firmly held belief that a promise is a promise, end of discussion.

But there will be other factors, other deterrents, such as **natural human indolence**. Love affairs can be hard work. Seeds have to be planted, and if they take root, they have to be nurtured under difficult circumstances. Rather like preparing an entry for the Chelsea Flower Show without letting anyone see you with a hoe in your hand. Who needs that kind of aggravation? Isn't life tiring enough as it is?

Then there is the **natural fear of rejection**. Your wife may find your spreading paunch attractive in a homely, comforting kind of way, but that girl with the legs in Telesales might laugh at it. She might say, 'Dinner? With *you*? You have to be kidding! Take my advice, Grandad, give dinner a miss for a few hundred weeks!' Or, what if you're not such a terrific lover as you hope you are? What if you're malformed and your husband never told you? What if you take another girl to bed and she falls asleep just as you go from your acclaimed set-piece into your Grand Finale? What if you do to Lulu what you usually do to Gwen, and Lulu calls the Vice Squad?

No, the whole concept of extra-marital how's-your-father is riddled with difficulties and worry. Far safer to stick with what you know. That, in a nutshell, is the thinking of thousands of married people who accept diminishing intensity as the *quid pro quo* of knowing exactly where they stand. A great many people would rather have safe, predictable sex than stage-managed nights of endless passion, and quite a few would rather play bridge.

This is wonderful when both partners feel the same way. **Monotony** is one of the most deprecated conditions in life, but those who knock it should recognise that many marriages thrive on it. And if you believe in fidelity but are bored witless, there are plenty of experts ready to give advice on how to prevent sexual *ennui*.

My friend Tom is still banging away with abandon after eighteen years of marriage.

I said, 'How d'ya do it, Tom?'

'We work at it,' he said. 'We set aside **Quality Time**.'

'Quality Time?'

'Yup. We block it out on the calendar. Then, we keep ourselves in good shape. We work out, we go easy on junk food and caffeine, we don't do drugs, Marcy has her legs waxed every five weeks, and we both floss religiously every morning and night.'

'Is that it?' I asked, feeling a bit overcome.

'Hell, that's only for starters!' he said. 'We do different

things all the time. We try different massage oils, mirrors, candlelight. Sometimes we do it in the back of the car. Anything to beat the gridlock! Last night I surprised her with an ocelot jockstrap.'

I had to ask. 'Did it work?'

'She said she'd have preferred it in black.' Tom is nothing if not honest. I think that's the real reason Marcy never looks at another man.

Then there are **the unfaithful**. Some who seem able to handle it, and many who definitely do not.

If a man is going to be unfaithful, he will usually have his first affair within five years of marriage. A woman is likely to do it later, often not until her forties.

When the reasons for an affair are revenge or boredom or terror about grey hairs, crows' feet and the passage of time, the prognosis is not good, for the affair or for the marriage. When the reason for an affair is that there is something irreparably wrong with the marriage, it can be the motive force that's needed to call an end to something bad and make a fresh start. Can be. Strangely, affairs often don't work that way. Many unhappily married people enjoy a series of love affairs but always retain a primary attachment to the partner they have grown to need and detest.

One of the first things people want to do when they've started an affair, is blab about it. They want to call up a good friend and say, 'If I don't tell someone in a minute I shall burst!' The good friend is about to become a casualty. He or she is about to be told the name, address and inside leg measurement of a secret. It is just about the shittiest burden you can dump on a friend. I mean, say, just say, Marcy did look at another man. Say she called me and said, 'Laurie, the most wonderful thing has happened! Meet me at the Cork and Bottle because I have to tell you!' So I meet her, and we share a bottle and guess what? She's having a fling. Marcy used to spell *fling*

A-D-U-L-T-E-R-Y, but now she spells it A-D-V-E-N-T-U-R-E.
It is three-quarters agony and one quarter bliss, and she's doing
it because Tom keeps going on business trips without her and
Hesketh makes her feel so alive! *Hesketh?* Yes! And what's
more, the affair is actually improving her marriage. Enriching it
by the hour.

All kinds of questions go through my mind as I order another
bottle. Like, is it true that what you don't know doesn't hurt
you? And should we bring Tom in on this and ask him whether
he's feeling enriched in any sense? Worst of all, what am I
going to say when Tom asks me, 'Did you know, Laurie?' and
it's obvious he already knows the answer?

I can't help thinking that when the penny drops, and Tom
realises he's the only person in the Northern Hemisphere to
have missed out on a raunchy conspiracy, he's going to have a
contribution or two to make to the long-running debate on
marital fidelity.

Marcy knows this too, but for the time being she has her
excuses ready. She's not *in love* with Hesketh because the
ground rules preclude it. As like as not he's married, too, and
intends to stay married. He made it clear from Day One that
tenderness and caring were prohibited. That they were two
grown-up people whose paths happened to cross and who
needed to get inside each other's knickers. And as she doesn't
want to lose him, Marcy has agreed to take her cue from him.
No love, no friendship. Just a rather cynical biological
encounter.

There may be trouble ahead. For one thing, Marcy may
break the rules and fall in love with Hesketh, and at that
precise moment he'll call and say, 'Don't call me. Ever again.'
She will then be consigned to a private hell-hole reserved for
married adventurers. A place where all grieving must be done
in silence. And whenever she sticks her head out to snarl at
Tom, he'll think, 'Funny how nasty these enriched marriages
can turn!'

118

Any marriage where there is a fundamental flaw is threatened by infidelity, but at least there is a kind of hope attached to the threat. If you have chosen the wrong partner and then meet the right partner, isn't that progress? Some people make fantastically good second marriages.

The greater danger is to good marriages. If a basically fine marriage is going through an indifferent patch and then gets dealt a blow, it may never pick itself up off the canvas. One love affair may not prove terminal, but it can change things for ever. A rot can set in, and what seemed like an act of great

119

audacity the first time, doesn't seem like such a big deal the next time, or the next. An affair may be right, it may be wrong, you need the benefit of hindsight to be sure. The only certainty is that it is dangerous to the *status quo*.

So I say, 'Marcy, you'll get in over your head and then he'll drop you.'

But she says I wouldn't think that if I knew Hesketh.

I say, 'You'll get caught.'

And she answers, 'We won't! We're so careful! We meet in Gunnersbury because absolutely nobody ever goes there, and we both wear dark glasses, and we have this clever signalling system for phone calls. By the way, Laurie, I told Tom I'm having dinner with you next Thursday, so could you please be out all evening in case he calls to check?'

That's the trouble with flings. No one's ever very sure what they're flinging, or what will happen if any of it hits the fan.

And what about **other kinds of infidelity**? Is it likely or reasonable that the person you marry should provide you with everything you will ever need in terms of companionship and stimulation? If you like to sing madrigals and she thinks madrigals are an exotic fruit from Thailand recently marketed by Tesco's, will it be infidelity every time you get together with other madrigal singers and live it up? Especially if some of them are lady madrigal singers. And if you are hopeless at listening to people, unless it's about car engines or Rugby Union, and your wife understands this and takes her talking elsewhere, to friends, some of whom may be men, is that infidelity?

It could be. Can married people have friends of the opposite sex? With great difficulty, more's the pity. The marriage has to be very good, very secure, the partners in it have to be big-hearted and certain of their own worth. If a marriage scores less than full marks on these points, *it* isn't a friendship, and if *it* isn't a friendship how can it support another friendship between a man and a woman? All these ways of being unfaithful without ever getting out of your armchair!

And we still haven't mentioned Saturday Football, Sunday Football, Coxed Eights, Tennis, Tennis Club Socials, Tennis Club Future Events Sub-Committee Meetings, religion, active membership of a political party, and golf! Any of which can keep a person absent and sadly missed from the marital home for longer than is just or fair. All infidelities of a sort, I would say. But if the faithless one won't be persuaded to spend more time at home, the abandoned partner always has the option of saying, 'I can't beat this, so I'll join it,' or, 'I can't beat this, so I'll join something else.'

This is not so when you are faced with **the most treacherous rival of all**. The mistress that can never be bested, the lover who can't be challenged to pistols at dawn. Age never withers her. She can demand whole weekends of undivided attention. She can get away with phone calls at midnight, use menaces to get quarts into pint pots and silk purses out of sows' ears, and refuse ever to understand the meaning of the word *No*. The heartless whore that calls herself Work. Sometimes she's called Oustanding Success at Work. Sometimes she's called Unemployment, or Retirement from Work. Makes little difference which alias she's using. *She's* the third party in the Eternal Triangle.

'Where the hell have you been! I cooked you lasagne and it's ruined.'

'I've been in a wine bar.'

'You've been in a wine bar entertaining a client?'

'No. I've been in a wine bar treating my toy boy as a sex object.'

'Don't lie to me! I called your secretary. She told me the Training and Resources meeting was over-running by hours!'

'She just said that to make trouble. Anyway, I told you not to call me at work. You want to know why I'm late? I'll tell you. I fell over this fabulous man in the bank. I dashed in to order those traveller's cheques and we collided with one another. I mean, this was a body that was too good to miss!'

'So?'

'So I invited him to drink champagne from my shoe after work.'

'Do you expect me to believe a story like that? Admit it! You've been working late!'

Retrospective Infidelity

This is probably the most ridiculous charge one partner can make against another, but it happens. You may be settled in for the duration, contented and convinced that you have made the wisest of matches, when your turtle dove bowls you a beamer: 'Who did you love before you loved me? For how long? And precisely what form did this love take?'

Personally I can never get excited about other people's memories, because I have memories of my own, when I can remember them, but I've heard of some real showdowns between husband and wife. Jealous rages because Janice Bottomley used to ride pillion on his motorbike. Black looks concerning Nigel Lorrimer, several pints of cider, and virtue lost on the back seat of a Ford Pop.

I used to think it was a male weakness, this contradictory desire to have a partner who has lost the rough edges of her sexual technique but who still has a cellophane wrapping. But the more I talk to men about what makes their wives sulk, the more I realise that women are just as guilty.

'No, go on, tell me. I'm very interested.'

'I can't remember that far back!'

'Well can you remember her name?'

'I think it was Anne.'

'And was she better looking than me?'

'She had nice hair.'

'Nicer than mine?'

'Different.'

'And you were really crazy about her?'

'I was very fond of her.'

'So if she had such fabulous hair, and you were head over heels in love with her, why didn't you marry *her*? You're obviously still carrying a torch for her! I mean, why don't you put an end to this whole charade and go and find her? Go on! Put a Personal Ad in *The Times*! I bet she's sitting around, combing her gorgeous flowing tresses, just waiting for you to call!'

'Ethel! Can we get on and enjoy our Golden Wedding Party, and discuss this later?'

Never rise to this kind of bait. Any one who talks like this is simply at a loose end and spoiling for a fight. If you do get drawn into one of these sessions, the only defence is amnesia, or the bare-faced lie, as in:

'Until I met you on the eve of my twenty-ninth birthday, I spent all my nights making balsa wood aeroplanes.'

or,

'Thornton Heath Tigers? What, *all* of them? No, there's been some mistake. Actually, now I recall, there was *another* girl called Xanthe Piggot du Bois, who was putting it about a bit at that time.'

════ **18** ════

Nine till Five

At a party recently I joined a circle of strangers and having introduced myself was staggered to be asked, 'And what does your husband do?' The person who asked me wasn't some crusty old buffer accustomed to seeing women embroidering fire-screens. She was a woman of my own generation. A married woman whose husband's salary and own inclination had encouraged her to be a full-time housewife. A very superior class of housewife, I'd guess. The kind who'd have time to polish the brasses and dust the top of the wardrobe. I was struck dumb and yet, easily within my memory, that was the norm. Women married, tiddled around with a bit of a job until the first baby, and then tiddled around a bit more after the last baby had grown up and time began to hang heavy. But **a career**? Not if you were serious about marriage. For a career you stayed single.

Well of course so much has changed. Now we have working mothers, role-reversal families, high-flying women, double-income couples who choose to remain childless, redundancy, two and a half million unemployed, *and* thousands and thousands of women who tiddle around with a bit of a job until the first baby and then . . .

Whichever way you cut it, someone in the marriage is perceived as the main breadwinner. This may have nothing at all to do with actual earnings. A man may be earning considerably less than his wife, but if there is even the tiniest chance of her getting pregnant, when the chips are down *his* income is the one that counts. The only way this is avoidable is where the wife does a job that she can continue, easily and independently, virtually without a break, through pregnancy, childbirth and several years of night feeds, chickenpox and school holidays that go on and on and on. Something like staying at home and writing books. Why didn't *I* think of that sooner?

Here is the score. We are still a million miles from wives' careers achieving equal status with husbands' careers. My own unrevolutionary theory is, that it will never happen. Biology just won't go away.

If you are childless and you both work outside the home, you are both susceptible to the vagaries of the job market. This may mean being willing to work unsocial hours, to study, or to pull up your roots and re-locate when asked. So if you've been offered Strathclyde and *she's* just been promoted to Head Office, Gillingham, what's going to happen? In most marriages what's going to happen is you're going to Strathclyde. Or, you're going to meet for alternate weekends in Nottingham. This has been known to work. Some couples manage very nicely working on different continents, but many do not, especially if they try to do it at the beginning of a marriage.

The **mobility problem** is where the first little sacrifice of career plans goes up in smoke.

The next hitch affects all couples, not just jet-setters who get exiled to Runcorn. **Energy**. Lack of it. You both work, you both come home tired. You have a house to run, family and friends to see, lives to live, and neither of you feels much like doing any of it.

Enter the **Working Wife**. She loads the washer-drier as she eats her muesli, shops in her lunch hour for light bulbs, Y-fronts, and frozen dinners, and when she gets home she has only to cook, wash, dry, iron, and write yet another shopping list, before showering, lacing herself into a silk basque and working through the next ten pages of *The Art of Feminine*

Lechery. All right, maybe I exaggerate a little. I will admit that now so many men have become **New Men** these working wives do get a few breaks. The odd plate wiped. The occasional meal microwaved. But still not a lot of chaps on the 5.20 to Basingstoke limbering up for three hours' ironing.

I make no apology for this outburst of female chauvinism. Men who help at all get recognition out of all proportion to the contribution they make. This is because most working wives are chumps. Any woman who rewards the washer-up of a few measly cups with instant canonisation wants her bumps feeling. No she doesn't. She's too tired.

Of course she is. She's servicing two people (at least) as well as doing her eight-hour stint at work, and trying to be a human being.

'I mustn't grumble,' she says, 'Mike usually does Sunday breakfast, and he always cuts the lawn.'

So let's hear it for Mike, ladies and gentlemen! Never mind about who changes the sheets, buys and wraps thirty Christmas presents, and stitches on loose buttons! He mows the lawn and sometimes grills a couple of sausages, so no one can accuse this man of dragging his feet. Mrs Mike, you see, is her own worst enemy, but I can't condemn her. The odds against her ever making any progress in this battle are so high, it's understandable that she can't be bothered to take aim. Eventually she'll either earn enough to pay someone else to service Mike, or she'll give up her career from sheer exhaustion. Whichever way it goes, Mike will never be any the wiser as to the function of a lavatory brush.

Will any married man who has ever come home from a hard day selling equities and cleaned a lavatory, please stand up?

The more successful a career becomes, the bigger the demands it makes. Erratic hours, weekends and holidays sacrificed, sometimes fortune, and even fame. Women cope with this happening to their husbands a lot better than men cope with it happening to their wives. For a woman, looking up and feeling proud seems quite natural. There is a tradition passed from mother to daughter that reflected glory is more seemly and becoming than hogging the spotlight yourself. It takes a lot of maturity and self-esteem for a man to feel this easy with the supporting role. Modest success is fine. A man will advertise some small achievement made by his wife and he'll do it with genuine pride, but if she turns into a World Beater, very likely he won't be able to live with it comfortably. Isn't *he* the one who should be Director of Public Relations UK, while *she* works three mornings a week in a wool shop? She may be doing well at something, and he may love her very much, but what if it proves to be the un-manning of him?

And so the arguments keep circling. If he has a career, what about her career. If *she* has a career, what about his career, dirty laundry, and psychological integrity?

And what if one of you wants to go out on a limb and be **a home-worker**? Worse even than the compulsive grafter who brings home papers, cuts short holidays, and installs a Fax machine in the bathroom, is the person who works at home. Sounds idyllic, doesn't it? Three hours a day freed for productive endeavour instead of fighting for your life on Southern Region? Someone always on hand to take in parcels and wait hours for the plumber to show up?

But ask anyone who is married to a home-worker and they will show you the other side of the coin. A picture of alternating indolence and manic activity, linked by marriage-wrecking episodes of self-loathing. Whole mornings spent wailing, 'It's no good! I can't do it! I should never have set up this business in the first place. I'm so lonely. No one ever puts their head round my door and invites me out for a few beers.' Followed by whole afternoons screeching, 'Just shut the door and go away! Do you have the faintest idea how busy I am? I have a completely impossible deadline to meet and I seem to be working in the middle of Piccadilly Circus! Will people kindly stop inviting me to the pub! *This* is my office, in case you hadn't noticed.'

People who work at home develop anti-social habits. They work in their dressing gown, they pick their nose, go for walks when they should be working, work when they should be sleeping, and occupy at least one room in the house with office clutter that cannot be tidied, dusted or even looked at without slighting the importance of the project in hand. They are there all day long, burning electricity, eating biscuits, and gobbling up telephone units, and still the lavatory doesn't get cleaned.

If someone wants to drop out of P A Y E, then what?

Young women often see having children as a means of **dropping out**, because child-rearing is an unstructured, unwaged career. Men collude with them in this myth. Shouldering the responsibility for earning all the money required must make a man feel very strong and very frightened all at the same time.

'You're going to make a wonderful mother! Go and put your feet up,' he says, but deep inside a small but nasty voice is whispering, 'It's not fair! I could make a go of pregnancy if someone'd give me the chance. I never wanted to be Features Editor! What am I doing here? I could push a pram. I could ride around in a pram. That's it! I'd make a terrific baby! Wonder if I could get a sabbatical. . . ?'

This is a delicate moment in any marriage. The loosening and the taking up of reins has to be carefully timed if the pleasure and excitement of the challenge isn't to be lost amongst the fear and resentment. Any man planning on having an identity crisis at work *and* children, should take care not to do both at the same time.

The upheaval caused to careers by having children does have one thing going for it. Society approves. People can be jolly decent about successful women while they are obliged to, but listen for the sigh of relief when she enrols for ante-natal classes and starts needing afternoon naps.

'Phew! At last! Now Dick can become a real man and we shan't have to watch ourselves for sexist solecisms!'

But there are other methods of dropping out that aren't nearly so acceptable. Some of them will get you pelted with rotten eggs. Like taking a substantial drop in salary to do something you consider worthwhile. Like sitting with your redundancy money in your hand, having a long, hard think about noses, grindstones and the meaning of life. Like trying to sail round the world with fifty cans of corned beef and a home-made coracle. Or becoming a student.

The point being that once you are married you're supposed either to do a *proper* job or become a housewife. Anything else is reckoned to be flaky behaviour and from a man, unpardonable.

'You are going to do *what*?'
'Paint.'
'Paint? The garden wall? Damian's bedroom? What?'
'Murals.'
'Murals. Seventeen years in bathroom fittings and you're going to paint murals?'
'And frescoes.'
'You realise we'll be finished with the Rotary Club! The Chamber of Commerce will wash their hands of you! Seventeen years in sanitary ware gone . . .'
'Down the drain?'
'Pass me my Valium!'

The moral of this story is, if you have dreams of lotus-eating you really have to do it before marriage or after many years of

130

it, when the children have grown up and gone, and you have nothing to prove.

The **commonest cause of marital breakdown** after a marriage has survived decades and won long-service medals, is a twenty-year-old-blonde who makes him feel so young, who makes him feel that spring has sprung.

The **next commonest cause** is retirement. A man who has been Someone, whose opinions counted and whose power was mighty to behold, who started early, finished late, wrote reports in his trunks on the beach at Biarritz, slept with the telephone under his pillow and was a totally inconsiderate bastard in all matters domestic and familial, suddenly becomes a different kind of bastard. He doesn't bother to shave. He pours his first drink too early in the day. And he trails around behind his wife like a newly-hatched chick. He has nothing to do. He can't help, because he doesn't know where the kitchen is and, anyway, after forty years who needs help like that? He can't call his friends because he never had time to make any. And the more the telephone doesn't ring with urgent requests for him to fly to Stuttgart and bring the Germans up to speed on a few things, the uglier he gets.

This is the time in a marriage when the career plans of a typical wife don't look so pathetic any more. She did a little of this, a little of that, had the children, dabbled a bit when they went to school, maintained at all times a strong network of friends, stretched herself further into middle-age, and whatever her other commitments, always touched base several times a day in the servicing and nurturing of her family. In this sense women never retire. And men probably envy them.

There is another factor in the career–marriage tug-of-war. Apart from how many hours a day it occupies and what it pays, there is the important question of **what the job actually entails**.

131

The marriage partners of police officers, doctors, sex idols, sewage operatives and astronauts will all tell you why.

Some jobs are easy to understand.

'I'd like you to meet Cyril. He's a lion tamer. And this is his wife Madge. She's a librarian and in the evenings she's a hooker. Tonight's her night off.'

We all know exactly where we stand with Cyril and Madge. But how often do you meet people who are so straightforward? How often do you ask a man what he does for a living, and half an hour later he's still telling you and you still don't know? Why is that? Is he under instructions from his wife?

'You tell *anyone* you sell hot dogs and I'm as good as on that train home to Mother.'

Or is it that there are a lot of people who don't really know what they do, married to another lot of people who don't know either? Do *you* know what your partner does? Are you sure? Do I? Sort of. He showed me a pile of computer print-out once, but my foot went dead, and then it was time for us to watch *EastEnders*.

Some scope for improvement here, wouldn't you say? Room for husbands and wives to understand better the skills and pressures of each other's working lives? Then, if a bimbo at a party asks you what your husband does, instead of choking with rage and ignorance on your canapé like I did, you can say 'He's out six days a week selling foreign real estate. I keep myself busy making loose covers and being President of the National Council for Civil Liberties, but I expect as soon as the bottom falls out of the time-share market I shall have him under my feet, in an old cardigan and three days' stubble. How's business with you?'

19
Time Out

Holidays can be the damnedest things. Every year you feel you should take one, and every year you end up thinking, 'Did *I* make this happen?'

Everyone who submits to a normal human quota of hard slog and drudgery needs time off. But the kind of holiday you need depends on the kind of drudgery you've been getting. This is the problem with married holidays. One of you wants to read Pericles, clock some Great Art and contemplate the wine-dark sea, and one of you wants to be silly with a beach ball.

Women are the do-ers in life, have you noticed? Never mind about the Pyramids and the Great Wall of China. I'm talking about more than a bit of bricklaying. Women love to be on the go. They like to shop and self-cater and gaze at bronzes of men in fig-leaves, before hurrying on to more shops. Women are heroic shoppers, especially in foreign currencies.

They also enjoy preparing for a holiday. They say they hate it but they're fibbing. They love buying sandals and reading Michelin Guides. They think very long and hard about sun oil and boarding kennels. For a woman, this holiday foreplay is as exciting as the thing itself.

Men are different. Bikini-waxing would never have caught on with men. They don't even look for their trunks until five hours before the flight leaves. Then they feel down the back of a drawer and drag out something evil and sandy, something the moths have chewed and coughed up, and they say, 'Well that's me packed!'

Once that plane touches down there are two varieties of

133

holiday-making husband. Those who are congenitally incapable of going twelve hours without calling the office, and those who like to do nothing. Doing nothing can include a little gentle diversion with a Frisbee or a jug of strawberry daiquiri, but that's about as far as it goes.

Marriage partners who pine for loaded In-Trays and smoke-filled committee rooms should be left at home. Don't waste your time trying to tempt them with pictures of palm trees. Do you want him keeping the glass-bottom boat waiting while he calls Dunstable collect? Do you really want to skinny-dip if the attaché case has to come along too? Of course you don't. Book a fortnight away with your mother and leave the following note on the mantelpiece:

There are 14 steak pies in the deep-freeze and 14 clean shirts in the closet. We don't have 14 dinner plates, so don't even consider it. Your Ventolin's in the bathroom. And the cat's name is Bill.

If you're the sort of people who believe you should re-charge your batteries side by side, it's sensible to start with some ground rules. There are married people who both want to take walking tours through Zimbabwe, but not many.

Some of us are night birds, some of us are larks. Some of us never get it together without a lot of black coffee and a brisk talking to. And this is only the beginning of a list of incompatibilities that can turn a holiday into a ten-round fight. What about beaches, and water? Plenty of decent people hate sand. And what about mountains? We don't all go troppo at the sight of snow-capped peaks, and yet it's generally agreed that if it's a holiday you're wanting, mountain air must be somewhere near the top of your priorities.

If you are married to someone who disagrees with you on every particular of geography and climate, you should take turns at choosing. Either that or go to Weston-super-Mare. No mountains, no ocean. No geography to speak of.

People change when they're on holiday. Some just get more entrenched. Normally they read one Mills & Boon a week. On holiday they read ten. Others go completely off the rails. They spend fifty weeks a year managing a building society branch office, but show them a beach and they can't stop leap-frogging, and digging replicas of Oulton Colliery. Men especially are prey to delusions of lithe athleticism. A man can lie around at home looking like two hundred pounds of rendered lard, but put a little sand beneath his feet and he develops a go-getting streak:

'We'll make a driftwood fire.'
'I don't see any driftwood.'
'This has always been your trouble, Cassie. You're so negative! We'll build a driftwood fire. Bivouac down here till the tide turns, then catch sand-eels and cook them over the flames.'
'Simon . . .'
'We'll wash the sand-eels down with a bottle of fizz, make

love under the stars, and sleep, till we're woken by the cry of the whimbrels.'

'Simon . . .'

'Yes, Cassie?'

'This is Pwllheli. It's Sunday. The champagne shops are all shut, Butlins have only let us out on a Day Pass, and there's a local bye-law against frightening the whimbrels.'

'Shit. Okay, we'll get a boat and sail across Cardigan Bay!'

Never agree to do anything in a boat if you're not 100 per cent happy about it. Unless you're at the Boat Show and someone is offering you a great deal of money. Boats are not things to mess with. Well, they *are* things to mess with. Some people do precious little else. But they are not things to pretend about. If you need to impress or appease someone, do it on dry land. Being a happy sailor is an instinctive thing. I have yet to be convinced that you can train someone to enjoy sailing, even if they have very good credentials. I come from a long line of one-legged seafarers, and the first two things I think when I get on a boat are (1) I'm getting off and (2) As I've not been allowed to get off, I shall certainly drown. This is nothing to be ashamed of. If the Lord had intended us to cross Cardigan Bay, he would have given us a keel instead of feet.

I know of a marriage between a sailor and a land-lubber. Each holiday brings them a little closer to the divorce courts.

'Walter, I'm going below.'

'You come back here. There's always something needs doing on a boat.'

'There's something needs doing on my bunk!'

'Damn it Margaret, we've planned to sail to Finistère and we're gonna do it if it kills me!'

'I'm going to be sick, Walter.'

'No you're not. It's all in the mind. Now go into the garage and fetch me the pliers.'

And so it goes. The world is full of married people who can't do their own thing. *Togetherness* is the name of the game.

On holiday? Of course we're on holiday — why else would we be in a dump like this?

Separate holidays are reckoned to be the beginning of the end. Give a man a bag of golf clubs and a sunhat and let him off the leading rein – who can say whether you'll ever see him again? Then there are Spanish waiters to worry about. And topless beaches, and leather shops that take Barclaycard. The whole concept of holidays apart is beset by risks, the chief one being that you will both enjoy yourselves so much you'll want to do it again. Marriage is not about this kind of self-gratification. Marriage is about compromise. Since *he's* not going to be allowed to walk the Pennine Way getting up to no good with the sort of girls you find in Youth Hostels, *she's* not going to be allowed to go to Minehead for two weeks of Creative Crochet and West Country gigolos. They'll go to Ramsgate together. Then they'll both be miserable. Pity really, isn't it?

20

Why Bother?

At the beginning of a marriage there are plenty of outsiders willing to wager on the likelihood of its surviving. They shake their heads gravely as the vows are exchanged and mutter, 'It'll end in tears. Kevin's always flat on his back under his car. He'll drive Sharon to drink.' What these Jeremiahs are overlooking is that one of the many reasons Sharon chose Kevin, was that he is in love with the inside of a very old Cortina. At the time of marriage she still finds it endearing that he likes to tinker. Or, if it's been a very long engagement, she is perhaps not as charmed by it as before and is making modest plans to control this eccentric behaviour. Either way she knows she's getting a man whose only cosmetic aid is a bumper tin of Swarfega. She has settled for this.

The survival of the marriage depends on other things. It depends on who Sharon and Kevin become. And what potholes open up beneath their feet. No one can make allowance in advance for some of the devastating events that can be the undoing of a marriage. Illness, injury, debt, unemployment, a death in the family, a birth, a re-birth even. Life may have been rubbing along nicely enough, and over-night change beyond recognition. Any survivor will tell you that major human tragedies ask more of marriages than many of them can give. Most of us, trying merely to survive the everyday irritations of a close relationship, don't know our own luck.

We marry because we feel safer in pairs. Society is arranged in such a way that to live alone or in some large indefinable

139

community is to be pitied or reviled. *Normal* people like a bit of company. Choose someone of the opposite sex, and not only do you have someone to warm your feet on in bed, you also have the raw material of procreation. Someone to bitch at *and* a stake in the future!

So we look around, we see the point of marriage, and start searching for someone who's free for the next fifty years. We choose another human being. Someone who will be neurotic, selfish, feeble, obsessive, aggressive, regressive and generally flawed in the best human tradition.

There is an old saying that opposites attract. I'm not so sure. At least, they may attract, but the attraction won't endure. If you're going to live with someone for the rest of your life, you don't want someone who'll keep breaking your rules. You want a partner who has nearly the same set of rules you do. You want a partner who will understand what makes you tick, and having understood you, give you permission to carry on existing. And that's not all. The other small favour we want our marriage partners to do us, is make us feel complete, happy and alive. But if they are to be capable of that, they're going to need strengths we can't find in ourselves. So ideally, we want to marry people who understand and accept us, play by the same rules, and have enough up their sleeve for a spot of extra cherishing, as and when required.

Amazingly enough, this is what a lot of us get. A deal is struck between a man and a woman without a word of the following conversation being spoken:

'Sharon, I am a basically unadventurous, home-loving scruff with a good heart, an inability to open up emotionally, and a thorough working knowledge of Ford engines.'

'That's all right, Kevin. What I don't know about cars I can make up for on Aran knitting patterns. In every other respect we are identical.'

'What about my need to be respected and nurtured all at the same time?

'No problem. I'm a similar case myself. Periodically I shall become deeply disillusioned about you as a provider, and resentful that my many acts of self-denial and caring go unsung. I shall tell you that you're all mouth and no balls . . .'

'. . . Then I'll put you in your place by reminding you how immature you are . . .'

'. . . and we'll patch things up over a nice bottle of wine!'

'Budweiser, Sharon! Not *wine*! Budweiser.'

'That's another thing. I'm going to smarten up your image.'

'You are? Am I going to enjoy it?'

'Who cares!'

Sharon and Kevin have the basis of **a survivable marriage**. Kevin wants to play the Male Lead, and Sharon wants to be best supporting actress. Like any supporting role, this requires strength. So Sharon is actually stronger than she shows, and probably stronger than she realises. Kevin is different. With him it's the vulnerability that's kept under wraps. He can pretend to be indestructible because publicly Sharon is doing the vulnerable bit – tears, panic, hysteria and so forth – and privately she's being a rock so Kevin can be a closet jellyfish. They complement and supplement each other's performance. This is the state of equilibrium reached by millions of happy, quarrelling couples. If that equilibrium is destroyed, the marriage changes and the people in it have to adapt. If they don't, **the marriage founders**. There are **two ways this commonly happens**:

The first is that people marry without knowing each other well. They marry before they are beyond the Best Behaviour stage in their relationship. I'm not talking about lovers who pretend they will never play Demis Roussos records or leave the top off the toothpaste. These are insignificant irritations. We all have them, we all deny them, and if *you* don't tolerate them in your partner, who else might he go off and irritate? When I speak of Best Behaviour I mean simple human interaction.

Some people are able to conceal part of their personality. They conceal it from themselves as much as from other interested parties. The trait that is concealed is not always a negative one. Sometimes we think it's in our own best interests to let a potentially powerful sleeping dog lie. But the point about concealment is, it takes effort. The kind of effort that can't be sustained for ever, and is easily abandoned when you're tired and weary and you think the person you're with won't notice. Marriage breeds familiarity, and with familiarity sleeping dogs wake up, change into cats, and get let out of the bag.

'I thought you were a feminist?'
'I'm sorry. It just slipped out.'

142

'Is there anything else I should know?'

'No. I'm fine. Everything's fine. Look at me! See how fine everything is!'

'I think there's something else I should know.'

'Okay. It's a fair cop. You got me bang to rights. My mother scares me, I can't handle anger, and spiders give me palpitations.'

'What else?'

'Ah shit! It's my hostility to women. I think it escaped about half an hour ago. This is terrible. I swear this has never happened before. What should we do? Should we call the police?'

'No, leave it to me.'

'Are you sure? Do you know what you're tackling? Do you have any idea how nasty it can turn?'

'Not as nasty as I can. Which way did it go?'

Quite big, important things can be concealed until a marriage begins to settle down, and the vigil each partner keeps over his secret personality is relaxed. The consequences can be horrific. They can be unremarkable. It's a question of degree. Some people are perfectly bearable even when they're being their most objectionable. And for some couples there is a silver lining to the blackest of clouds. There are trade-offs to be made. When one partner is behaving badly, the other will appear close to saintliness. Living with an utter bastard is the easiest way for anyone to feel like a paragon of good works *and*, best of all, it gives you the excuse to be a bastard yourself. You don't have to do it right away. You can save it for some other time. You're in credit, that's all that matters.

'Grow up! Look at me! This is how a proper grown-up person should behave!'

'Shan't! It's my turn to be the baby today, or have you forgotten?'

'Right. You've asked for this. It may be your turn today, but you wait till it's my turn. Oh boy! I am going to bring a whole new meaning to the word *immature*.'

Couples like this often split up. But sometimes they need each other too much to divorce. They may not be very happy together, but each of them needs someone, and no one else would have them. The marriage survives, fed on vitriol.

When one partner withdraws from the game or changes the rules, survival is less likely. This is **the other way a marriage fails**. The people in it need to change, and they can't let each other. They're the kind of people who dislike *all* change. They were just born that way. They come from those kind of families, perhaps. And it's one of the reasons they chose each other in the first place. Sharon and Kevin were both unadventurous home-loving creatures, remember? Their eyes met, the world stood still, and they couldn't wait to go out and dig themselves a little rut. But that was yesterday. Tomorrow, Kevin may want to soften up a little, or Sharon may get bored being the frightened baby girl, and yet each has a vested interest in keeping things the same. To change is always hard work, and who needs that?

No one is better placed than Sharon to let Kevin grow, and no one is better placed than Kevin to give Sharon the green light. But sadly they may not make it. The more adaptable they both are, the better their chances of re-drawing the marriage to accommodate the people they become. If they dig their heels in – because why upset everything after ten long years and just when they've got a new carpet and curtains to match – they end up with something unsatisfactory. A marriage where each pretends things are the same as they ever were.

But if neither of them wants to pretend, and neither of them wants to accommodate, war is declared. Every new development sees one of them making an official complaint and demanding their money back. These are the kind of marriages where men confide their hopes and fears to barmaids they just met, and women read their Open University textbooks in the lavatory. Both would do better married to someone with a big enough heart to let them grow, or let them *be*. *That's* what it's about. Things like who should wash the frying pan, and whether it's irresponsible to have a £50 ante-post bet on the Two Thousand Guineas *without discussing it first*, are details. They can seem important briefly, but they're not going to impede a healthy circulation in a marriage. Saying, 'I'm not going to let you be stronger because if you get stronger you may realise I'm not so strong as I'm cracked up to be and then you'll despise me,' is like putting on a tourniquet and leaving it. The change won't go away. Thwarted, it may go underground, or it may just keep nibbling away until it finds a different place to break out. That's the way it is with change.

You have a choice. You can get out, walk away from it, maybe try your luck with another partner. Or you must go with the flow. You have to be big, be generous, be *enabling*. Even to people who switch channels without asking.

Why bother? You've got me there. Why bother to do anything that doesn't clear you £15,000, tax free? Why bother relating to other human beings at all? Why not just get yourself up to a hermit's cave and let the species die?

How about, because relating to another person, one to one, makes you better, rounder and less judgmental, not forgetting flexible, resilient, nicer, and a little wiser? How about, because the world could do with all the nice, wise people it can get? How about, 'Live and let live! If I can stay married to Vera for twenty-five years I can sure as hell live with the Russians. Come to think of it, if I can stay married to Vera, I can probably live with the Martians!'

Call it survival through sustained niceness, if you like. Next stupid question?

21

And Finally,
a Word from the Stars

Astrology, as we all know, is a load of old bunk, because the sun is ninety-two million miles away from the earth, and even little Mercury is thirty-six million miles away from the sun and well, can you really believe any of that stuff?

But we do all like to take a sly look, and then say things like, 'Well my Albert is Pisces and he signed the Pledge when he was fourteen. He won't even have a sherry at Christmas.'

Then there are people who consult astrologers the way the rest of us watch weather forecasts. Except that they feel they can rely on what they're told. When it comes to choosing a husband or a wife, astrology is a factor some people dare not overlook. Whether the matches they make are any happier than those left to blind chance, it is impossible to say – happiness isn't at the top of everyone's marriage agenda anyway. But they may take some comfort, on the mornings they find themselves eating breakfast opposite the Creature from the Black Lagoon, in the knowledge that at least it doesn't have Leo in the ascendant.

Here, then, are all the mistakes you can ever make and blame on the solar system.

Aries
March 21st to April 20th

Humility? Tact? Patience? From a *ram*? Forget it. Candour?
Certainly. Energy? I get tired just thinking about Aries. The
ram's favourite mode of travel is Fast-Forward. This means
that his temper, which can be foul, is short-lived. The typical
Arien is a two-year-old child. He keeps trying to climb up the
back of the chair, and he keeps falling off, and he won't be
stopped or helped, and he really needs his potty but the
climbing and falling are far more interesting, and then he
finally makes it to the top, piddles all over the cushions, and is
convinced everyone will want to congratulate him warmly.

Aries is a very male sign. Which is why an Arien woman can
exist without a man better than any other female. Don't try
helping her on with her coat, or lighting her cigarette. She'll
beat you to it. And if you're shy about proposing, you can leave
that to her as well. But if you play the lovesick wimp to her
Scarlett O'Hara, the only thing she'll propose is that you pack
your bag and leave.

Taurus
April 21st to May 20th

Taurus is the Bull. Actually, Taurus is Sitting Bull. You like
passivity? Enjoy! Light the fuse on this one and you will only

have a matter of weeks to retire to a position of safety. These are excellent people to shack up with if you are attracted to farmyards. Nice, clean farmyards. A loft in Docklands is a bit too flash and a bit far removed from the earth to appeal to a Taurean. Obvious really. A bull in a high-rise? Only a non-Taurean would seriously entertain such a silly idea. Taureans are sensible.

A Taurean woman is no fluffball. She is restrained and practical. She works at two speeds – Steady, and Very Steady Indeed. There's only one way you can go badly wrong with Taurus, and that is by behaving like an impecunious slob. Use Lifebuoy soap.

Gemini
May 21st to June 20th

Gemini is twins. Gemini *are* twins? They can even be triplets. It can be like being married to a crowd scene. They never stand still. They move fast, talk fast, think *very* fast, and change their opinions and plans every half hour. It is impossible to find out what a Gemini truly thinks about anything, *except* that they happen to have, or know where they can get, the very thing you need. A Gemini could flog sand to an Arab.

The most comfortable way to live with a Gemini is to expect them when you see them. Male or female, they are supremely restless and moody. Also charming. They are not a wise sign to marry young. Such a big decision made early in life is a racing cert for the divorce courts. But if you choose one that's nicely matured, and you're content to live without any certainties in your life, marriage to Gemini is the only way I know of enjoying polygamy without breaking the law.

Cancer
June 21st to July 22nd

If you can live with the moody blues you'll do fine. Crabs can be deeply depressing people. Weeping, wailing, sulking. Then they come out of it and bite your head off. Shifty too. They pretend they're not interested in things, and then scuttle sideways and make a quick grab.

This is terrible. There must be something friendly I can say about crabs. Well they're not extravagant. When they fall in love they fall hard and hold on tight. And they love to stay home. Also to pay the rent on time, and check every item on the till receipt at Sainsbury's.

Crabs have intense relations with their mothers. This is putting it mildly. Worship or total alienation are the norm. Best to check which, before you tell a mother-in-law joke to Cancer.

Leo
July 21st to August 20th

Prepare yourself for amateur dramatics. Lions are always plagued by weaklings and idiots, and to be perfectly honest they can't have too much of it. They are staggeringly generous with money, help and advice, and they are brilliant at directing ops from a sun-lounger.

Tom cats are gallant and sentimental. They are also jealous. They like total female submission, and to know exactly where you are every minute of the day. If you are planning a career that will take you to the other side of the world at short notice without *him*, you are in for a lot of aggravation.

A lioness is a big woman. I am talking soul here, not body. She makes a good patroness. Holding court is her best sport. Never try to beat her at it. Of course, flattery will get you pretty well everywhere.

Virgo
August 21st to September 20th

I was trying to think if I had ever known a Virgo. Perhaps if I spent more time in libraries. . . ?

Virgos are neat, quiet and methodical. They don't care for vulgarity. I *knew* there had to be a reason I didn't know any. We all have habits, but Virgos only have sensible ones.

If you can get a Virgo boy even interested in a romantic relationship, you are nearly home free. But you cannot lure him away from chastity by hot pursuit or blatant seduction. He will only be tempted by a woman of pure intent.

In female Virgos, passion has been surgically removed and replaced by perfectionism. These girls are sticklers. And worry! You need never bother to do it again. She'll do it for you and make a much better job of it than you would. Life can be one long party with a virgin.

Libra
September 21st to October 20th

You seriously want to spend the rest of your life with a kitchen utensil? Okay. Like all scales, Librans spend more time unbalanced than they do balanced. This is the sign of the Devil's advocate. An honourable profession, and someone has to do it. But it is also the sign of the Barrack Room Lawyer (*see* 'Manwatching'). Never preface a remark to a Libran with, 'Of course there can be no doubt that . . .' unless you have several hours to spare.

You will never want for advice with a Libran husband. Your problem will be getting him to decide which way to jump. Beware of marrying a wavering Libra who is prepared to go through with the wedding sooner than upset the apple cart.

If you marry a Libran girl and are too easy-going to argue with her, don't worry! She'll argue with herself. What's more, she'll be scrupulously fair about the outcome.

Scorpio
October 21st to November 20th

Scorpions have had a very bad press. They are introverted, often silent. Talkative people find this unnerving. Then again, they are reputed to be explosively passionate. This also makes people nervous. Personally, I cannot see that this need be a problem unless you plan to spend your marriage playing poker or remaining celibate. As for the legendary sting – Scorpions are as likely to sting themselves as they are to harm anyone else.

They have surface cool and white-hot insides. They like to live well – an attic, with a diet of bread and water, is not really a Scorpio scene – and they are never better than when the referee has just counted them out. Remember the old phoenix from the ashes trick?

Scorpionettes do not make good bimbos. Hell hath no fury, if you sup with the Devil, etc, etc. And don't pry. Private means *private*.

Sagittarius
November 21st to December 20th

Sagittarians are full of drive, but you don't often see them with diplomatic plates on their car. They regularly open the mouth before engaging the brain. If an Arien is like a two-year-old who won't be beat, a Sagittarian is like a seven-year-old, galloping round the garden being a pretend horse, yelling comforting words to everyone she passes. Like 'Love the frock! Stops you looking so fat!'

They carry optimism to dimensions normal people cannot imagine. They're the kind of men who buy worked-out gold mines and never give up. Or only give up in order to move on to another useless hole in the ground. Essential equipment for marriage to one of these characters? A set of suitcases.

Female Sagittarians get restless too. They often get labelled as loose women, but they're not. They just don't like staying home and mopping floors when they might be out there, hiring Carnegie Hall for a one-woman comedy show. Can be very funny, but beware the hind legs.

Capricorn
December 21st to January 20th

Capricorn is a goat. What do goats do? I'll tell you. They climb the impossible and eat the inedible. They are as tough as old boots. Anything thought of as burdensome and frustrating by ordinary people – such as living at home with Mother until you're thirty – they take upon themselves with a sober sort of pleasure. Never show a Capricorn a short cut or a soft option. They prefer to plod dutifully on. *Noblesse oblige* with horns.

You appreciate irony? Marry a goat. Preferably a mature one. Understand that you will also be marrying his family, every last cousin of it, and be sure to buy a Year Planner so he can block out time for visiting aunts, doing the accounts, and sex.

Nanny goats don't like aimless flirtation. They like to know a chap's intentions. And they too improve with keeping. When they're young they look middle-aged. When they're middle-aged they blossom.

Aquarius
January 21st to February 20th

Aquarians are non-conformists. Oddballs to a man. Pairing up with mortals is a constant headache to them. They are tolerant of everyone and everything in a vague, distracted way, but they are difficult to pin down. Their minds are always away with the fairies, so any arrangements you make, like the time of your wedding, will be interpreted as optional guidelines. Water-bearers never see anything on face value. They see mystery and complications where there are none. And germs! These boys are into hygiene in a big way, let me tell you. Marriage to a Jewish Aquarian will require sterile conditions as well as a kosher kitchen. Never breathe near his toothbrush.

And an Aquarian girl is no passion puss either. But, you can take her anywhere and she won't let you down. Dancing on tables isn't her style. Neither is lending you a fiver till Friday, or telling you a lie. Telling you a half-story maybe, but a lie, never.

Pisces
February 21st to March 20th

Definitely not of this world. While goats climb the Eiger, North Face only, fishes go with the flow. It's hard to interest them in where the next meal is coming from, or what they're going to do with their lives. Unless they can examine the situation through the bottom of a glass. They are gentle souls, untainted by beastly ambition, and sadly prey to the demon drink.

Piscean men have a talent for missing the boat. Too busy listening to people's confidences and trying on dreams for size. Never marry a fish hoping he'll improve with keeping because he won't.

A Piscean girl is a lot of girl. She is the Unreconstructed Twinkie (q.v.). Soft and compliant, she will never nag a man. At least, not until after she's married him. Then she'll do it very sweetly. Frequently, meaningfully, but terribly sweetly.